Color
saves the day

Color
saves the day

Lucianna Samu
Photography by Mark Samu

CREATIVE HOMEOWNER®, Upper Saddle River, New Jersey

COLOR SAVES THE DAY

SENIOR EDITOR	Kathie Robitz
SENIOR GRAPHIC DESIGNER	Glee Barre
JUNIOR EDITOR	Angela Hanson
PHOTO COORDINATOR	Mary Dolan
DIGITAL IMAGING SPECIALIST	Frank Dyer
INDEXER	Schroeder Indexing Services
COVER DESIGN	Glee Barre
FRONT & BACK COVER PHOTOGRAPHY	Mark Samu

CREATIVE HOMEOWNER

VICE PRESIDENT AND PUBLISHER	Timothy O. Bakke
ART DIRECTOR	David Geer
MANAGING EDITOR	Fran J. Donegan
PRODUCTION COORDINATOR	Sara M. Markowitz

Manufactured in the United States of America

Current Printing (last digit)
10 9 8 7 6 5 4 3 2 1

Color Saves the Day, First Edition
Library of Congress Control Number: 2009927515
ISBN-10: 1-58011-475-X
ISBN-13: 978-1-58011-475-2

4339 #211   05/10

CREATIVE HOMEOWNER®
A Division of Federal Marketing Corp.
24 Park Way
Upper Saddle River, NJ 07458
www.creativehomeowner.com

Planet Friendly Publishing
✓ Made in the United States
✓ Printed on Recycled Paper
Text: 10%   Cover: 10%
Learn more: www.greenedition.org

GREEN EDITION

dedication

This book is dedicated to all who believe there's a place in their

home for each and every color they truly love.

acknowledgments

I wish to thank everyone at Creative Homeowner who made this

book possible, especially Kathie Robitz for her unwavering support.

Many thanks to my friend and husband, Mark Samu, for his daz-

zling photography and computer lessons, Peter for his colorful

feedback, Lucille for her wonderful dinners, and Joe for his cama-

raderie. I wish also to thank those who have graciously allowed us

to photograph their lovely homes. And finally, a most heartfelt

thanks to the designers and architects whose tireless pursuit of

the perfect palette is an inspiration to us all.

contents

introduction

Did you know that most people say their favorite color is blue? Then why are there so many white houses? This is just one of the burning issues I've tried to either resolve or explain in *Color Saves the Day*. If you're one of those people who likes color, but you're a little timid about living with it, this book is for you.

And if you're one of those people for whom there is never too much color, this book is for you, too. What I try to show in the pages that follow is that there is a real practical application of color that goes beyond your likes and dislikes.

Starting in Chapter 1, "Getting to Know Color," you'll find a few basic but important facts about color that are the foundation for any successful scheme. You'll see how colors influence one another and which ones work together harmoniously.

Chapter 2, "Exploring the Options," gets down to the heart of the matter: what do you want your color scheme to be? Are you a tiny bit kooky, unabashedly traditional, or a little of both? Here's how to put colors together that create mood and telegraph something about who you are.

Next, we get physical. Chapter 3, "Architectural Color," shows you how to alter or enhance space visually with color. Forget about blowing out the roof or lowering the ceiling. Projects such as those are expensive. Adding or changing a room's color is, well, cheap. And talk about saving money! Go to Chapter 4, "Color for Now," to see why you don't necessarily have to buy new furniture to update a room. Get with the times using fresh new colors.

Now I know there are people who don't have to be coaxed into the world of color. For those folks, Chapter 5, "Extreme Color," will provide a tour of some over-the-top palettes, as well as unexpectedly successful color pairings. For people at the opposite end of the spectrum, Chapter 6, "For the Color-Shy," will assuage your fear of using color, I assure you. If not, this chapter has plenty of information about—white! If you're a diehard white loyalist, you've got to read this one.

Of course, when anyone thinks about color in the home, the first thought is about paint. Some people love to paint, but those of you who don't won't believe that for a minute. For anyone who has ever painted around a bulky piece of furniture rather than move it—and those who just do not want to do it at all—Chapter 7, "Effortless Color," has some ideas for introducing color to a room without ever lifting a paintbrush.

Finally, Chapter 8, "What's in the Fore-cast?," offers a look at palettes that are not only wow for now but good to go for the new decade. If you can never be cutting-edge enough, this one's for you.

But that's not all, folks. Check out "Swatch-O-Rama," on page 160, which is the world of paint-color chips in a nutshell. Don't leave home without it—especially if you're going to the paint store or home-improvement center where you can make sure your match is perfect.

CHAPTER 1

Getting to

sometimes even

Know Color

a little bit says a lot

What's your favorite color? According to color authorities, most people over the age of 50 will answer "blue" about 80 percent of the time, followed by "yellow." If you pose the question to people between the ages of 25 and 50, chances are good that the answer will be split 50/40 in favor of blue over green, with purple making up the largest part of the remaining 10 percent. And when these people don't like blue, green, or purple, they usually pick yellow, too. It seems that only a few people favor orange, and even fewer prefer brown. At least that's what adults say—kids tell another story. Very young children tend to be noncommittal. How about you?

A SPLIT-COMPLEMENTARY SCHEME of a blue-green paint color for the wall and purple floral accents creates a fresh look for this room.

Living with Color

While some 20 years of color consulting doesn't equate with a scientific study, my experience with clients, family, and friends has revealed some interesting things. For one, most people can name a favorite color, but when it comes down to it, they can't commit. Even when I've conducted my "research" with the most sophisticated visitors to my home, the discussion often leads to a divisive and knotty conversation about color and how to use it. Case in point: I sometimes ask guests to choose their favorite room in the house—by color. Can you guess what happens? That's right, they can't do it. Why? Because their favorite room is usually not the one that features their favorite color.

So what is the problem? Why is it that confirmed blue lovers don't sleep in blue bedrooms, and why do green lovers gravitate toward neutrals? Why am I, a color enthusiast with a personal palette that borders on the ridiculous, a staunch defender and lover of all things orange and persimmon, serving dinner on white plates in an off-white dining room? The answer is simple: loving a color is one thing; living with it is something else.

OK, so my dining room is white and so are my plates. But dinner guests are greeted by a bouquet of Sonia roses the color of orange marmalade; the table is set with accent pieces that reflect my penchant for orange; and my less-decisive nature is sated by an ever-changing palette of tableware that reflects my mood of the moment. If you are a devout color lover, there's always a way to have it in your life.

CAREFULLY CHOSEN blue accents introduce a modulated level of color to keep this bedroom, left, quiet and restful.

POP GOES THE COLOR on my dining room table, where orange roses add color to the meal.

COLOR MAY COME FROM MANY SOURCES even mundane items, such as glassware or book jackets, left. Be careful that they don't clash with your palette.

UNDERSTATEDLY ELEGANT gray looks modern and sophisticated in the room below. Just a few colorful accents add more personality.

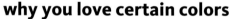

Another means to a colorful home, then, is to tell your personal color story, but not necessarily on the walls. If you're lucky to be starting fresh, take advantage of the opportunity by exploring all of the colors that appeal to you. Look for exciting ways to express your preferences in fabric, art, and accessories. Just keep in mind that you may have to overcome some color bias to ground a palette—pairing gray with a vivid accent, for example, or using several shades of brown in a room with lots of blue. Remember that avoiding certain colors can leave your rooms feeling cold. Little touches of cool gray or once-scorned acorn brown may be more enticing than you would have believed. And you may find that using buttery oranges, hot pinks, and persimmon with wild abandon is freeing after all.

why you love certain colors

There are places in your imagination and memory that hold fast to colors you have associated with pleasure. For many, these are childhood remembrances—a favorite yellow blanket with mint green satin trim or that first pink patent-leather "big girl" purse. Therefore, recognizing an affinity for certain colors is a logical way to begin planning a palette for your home. But keep in mind that your negative color prejudices occupy your color memory as well. Not surprisingly, the suggestion of such colors tend to elicit strong language and near visceral loathing. As a color planner and enthusiast, I can attest to the fact that negative color associations can cause you the most trouble when you're planning your home's color scheme.

BROWN DOESN'T ALWAYS WIN popularity contests, but you have to admit that combining several dark and light shades, above, is warmly appealing. Used as an accent color in pillows, left, and on the room's window treatment, right, a cool, pale blue—picked up from the art—brings subtle color into the space and relieves all of the browns without detracting from them. Blue and brown are always a successful pairing.

making a choice

Subtle environmental and physiological influences drive color preferences. Most significant is a phenomenon called "color constancy." The brain learns early that soil is brown, oceans are blue, and leaves are green. As children, our learning and cataloging of these constancies is reinforced by life experience. While the eyes can obviously discern each variation of these "norms," often the brain, in order to simplify things, overrides lighting conditions, compensates for distance and orientation of the objects in the viewer's field of vision, and presents a rational, albeit nearly preconceived, assessment of what you see. These associations are where the psychological connotations you assign to certain colors take shape—and many of them stick.

A RELAXING, REJUVENATING SCHEME is a perfect choice for a master bedroom, below, where the cares of the day can be forgotten. The designer, Lynn Gerhard, carried over the color of the bedding to the mantel, right, which displays matching pottery.

Talk the Talk

Some colors can be described as "warm" or "cool." Warm colors, such as yellow, advance, making space feel cozy. On the other hand, cool colors, such as blue, recede, which makes a space appear more open or airy. That's the most basic lingo. There are other terms you may hear bandied around concerning color. However, it does not help to know the difference between **hue, intensity,** and **value** if you're not sure whether you'd like a room to be blue or green.

Hue is merely the name of the color—blue is a hue; green is a hue; and so on. **Shade** refers to a change made to a color by the addition of black. For example, navy blue is a shade of blue. On the other hand, **tint** refers to change made to a color by the addition of white. Powder blue is, therefore, a tinted blue.

Value is the term that is used to indicate where a color falls on the gray scale—essentially it refers to the lightness or darkness of a color. Powder blue has a light value; navy blue has a dark value. **Saturation** is the brightness or dullness of a color. It's a word used interchangeably with **chroma,** a perception of the intensity of the pigment, rather than the color itself. For example, cyan is a saturated blue, while navy blue is not. Then there's **intensity,** which is similar in a way to saturation. Actually, it's an assessment of how pure a color appears. More gray makes it less intense.

"I look for shades of color that relax and rejuvenate at the same time. The accents can add the needed contrast, but for the most part, people tend to like walking in and feeling uplifted and calmed," says Lynn Gerhard of Gerhard Design.

There is some merit to having a general understanding of these color concepts, although you will not need to master them to make your way through this book. I have taken the liberty of discussing color in a language more in keeping with designer Ann Stillman O'Leary of Evergreen Interiors, who says "I live in a place that has many gray days, and in the winter the arc of the sun is short. I use warm colors, such as pumpkin and variations of yellows and golds, to 'paint the sunlight' into my rooms." Get the picture?

what color do you really want it?

THERE'S A PRICELESS SCENE in the classic old movie, *Mr. Blandings Builds His Dream House,* wherein Mrs. Blandings tries to explain to the house painter what colors she has chosen for various rooms. It goes like this:

"I want it to be a soft green, not as blue-green as a robin's egg, but not as yellow-green as daffodil buds. Now, the only sample I could get is a little too yellow, but don't let whomever does it go to the other extreme and get it too blue. It should just be a sort of grayish-yellow-green. Now, in the dining room, I'd like yellow. Not just yellow; a very gay yellow, something bright and sunshiney. I tell you, Mr. PeDelford, if you'll send one of your men to the grocer for a pound of their best butter, and match that exactly, you can't go wrong!

"Here is the paper we're going to use in the hall. It's floral, but I don't want the ceiling to match any of the colors of the flowers. There's some little dots in the background, and it's these I want you to match. Not the little greenish dot near the hollyhock leaf, however, but the little bluish dot between the rosebud and the delphinium blossom. Is that clear?"

"Now the kitchen is to be white. Not a cold, antiseptic hospital white, a little warmer, but not to suggest any other color but white. Next, it's the powder room. Here I want you to match this thread. Don't lose it as it's the only spool I have, and I had an awful time finding it! As you can see, it's practically an apple red. Somewhere between a healthy winesap and an unripened Jonathan."

Phew! It was great movie dialogue, but in real life, Mrs. Blandings may have had an easier time describing her wish list if she were familiar with the language of color. Then again, maybe not!

FEEL THE WARMTH from the color palette designer Ann Stillman O'Leary chose to brighten a room that gets gray northern light.

The Color Wheel

All of this "theoretical" discussion brings us to the **color wheel**—a fixed, circular arrangement of colors that reveal their relationship to one another. This is where our color conversation really begins, starting with the **primaries**—red, yellow, and blue. All other colors are made from these three. Mixing red and yellow, for example, produces a **secondary** color, in this case, orange. Mixing together one secondary and one primary color, such as blue and green, will produce a blue-green. This is called a **tertiary color**, and turquoise is an example. There are six tertiary colors. In addition to blue-green, there is yellow-orange, red-orange, red-violet, blue-gviolet, and yellow-green.

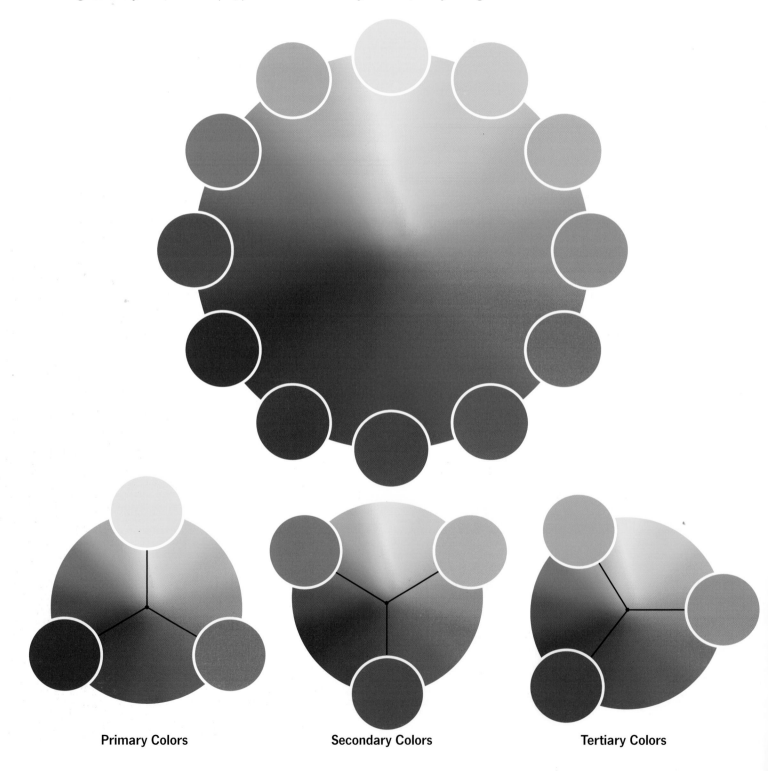

Primary Colors   **Secondary Colors**   **Tertiary Colors**

color wheel relationships

Colors such as yellow-green and red-violet oppose one
another on the color wheel, so they are **complementary.**
The value of either color will have an effect on your perception of the arrangement. Choosing a yellow-green and a red-
violet of equal saturation will enhance the brilliance of each
hue while producing a balanced, harmonious combination.

**MIX 'N MATCH is the
theme, and this wallcov-
ering, with its pretty
cool and hot pinks
accented with a yellow-
green, is a perfect
example of how pleas-
ing a complementary
scheme can be.**

Complementary Colors

Colors that are adjacent on the color wheel—blue and green, for example, or green and yellow—are called **analogous.** Complex analogous palettes can include as many as five consecutive colors. Using blue, blue-green, green, and yellow in the same room can be lovely. Now, if you added a bit of purple, or even worse orange, the pleasing analogous scheme would turn into quite a mess indeed. A good rule to follow for an attractive analogous scheme is to use no more than two **primary** colors.

A **split-complementary** scheme is made up of three colors—one complementary and two analogous. Lively and diverse, split-complementary schemes are exhilarating. Vary-

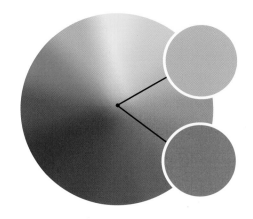

Analogous Colors

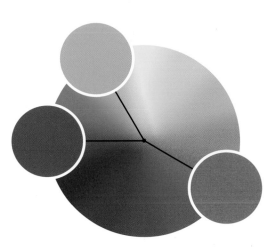

Split-Complementary Colors

ing the value of the colors can produce either soft or dramatic results.

Monochromatic schemes are based entirely on various tints and shades of a single color. Monochromatic neutral schemes with shades and tones of beige, gray, brown, black, and white could technically be described otherwise. However, this collection is generally accepted as a monochromatic neutral palette. (Black is actually the absence of all color; white is the presence of all color.)

While all of this "techy" talk is instructive and relevant to color in our lives and in our homes, in the end, none of it will have any great effect on your wish to own a sofa the color of terra verde or a living room that's painted a breathtaking shade of Italian ochre. But certainly you can train your eye to see the differences between yellow ochre and saffron, lemon and golden yellow. And with a few rules to bend, you will be able to build enough confidence to express your color personality. The only other things you need are an idea, a place to start, and a few good colors. Let's begin.

OFF-WHITE ON THE WALLS, opposite, allows a lively combination of colors—green, green-blue, and a violet-red (purplish pink)—to make its whimsical statement tastefully.

YELLOW-ORANGE AND ORANGE-RED form an analogous color scheme in this room, above right.

VARIOUS SHADES OF GRAY, right, look restful in this monochromatic scheme for a master bedroom.

CHAPTER 2

Exploring
What do you want

the Options

your home's color | scheme to say?

While gathering my ideas for this book, I made a long list of words I thought could be useful to describe particular colors—**kooky, pearly, playful, grassy, shimmery, muddy, and salty,** to name a few. Should every color name end in "y," I wondered? No, that's optional, I decided, moving on to **peaceful, chic, traditional, mod, tropical, and adventurous.** Then a larger question took shape: how is a color "tropical" in the first place? Does everyone sense that quality in magenta, or is it just me? Hmm. **The language of color** expresses more than that, starting with what it says about you and how you think the rooms in your house should look and feel.

UPDATED FOR TODAY, earthy green and brown with orange accents look chic in this contemporary living room. The repetition of circles in various patterns helps to put a modern spin on the design.

PLAYFUL COLORS, inspired by glass jars of confection, accent this media and game room, left, and put everyone in the mood for fun. Bright chartreuse green upholstery on the stools and banquette reinforce the soda-shop theme.

WHAT A SWEET IDEA. Iridescent glass, mosaic multicolor tiles carry a whimsical, candy-round message on the backsplash, below. They look delicious!

"Color should invite you into a room, ask you to have a seat and stay a while,"
—Susan Calabria/Noli Design

Color's vocabulary can be fueled by your travels and limited by your personal likes and dislikes. Like any language, it isn't universal; there are "colloquialisms" and "dialects," and you may choose to speak it with passion or reserve. Either way, a conversation begins the minute you bring colors into a room. It's up to you to encourage your ochre, viridian, cobalt, russet, or vermillion visitors to break into song.

If color is the invitation to sit, the excitement created by the combination of colors pictured above is likely to invite you to stay put long after the candy bowl is empty. Walking into this room, you're not exactly sure whether you want to eat, play, or just sit down and take in every bit of it.

The banquette and the stools in this modern-day game and media room are upholstered in chartreuse green. Overall, the space feels nostalgic and looks delicious with colors inspired by all of the candy on display in glass jars. Reminiscent of an old-fashioned ice cream parlor, the entire space looks good enough to eat!

What's the Vibe?

More than a theme, borrowing a palette and reinforcing the combination to support a design creates a palpable energy in a room. Some colors are more energetic than others.

Designer Maria Billis of Maria Billis Design, says, "The key to using color in a room is not only finding one that you love but having an awareness of the energy it creates." Red, for example, has a universally energetic connotation.

Conversely, colors that seem to be instinctively perceived, generally, as pretty, serene, and peaceful will create a sense of those qualities in a room. Most people associate sky blue, hazy gray, misty pink, and all pastel colors with an ethereal, even otherworldly, environment.

"I love roses, mauves, and soft browns. The combination creates a serene, harmonious, and soft space," says Evelyn Chin of EC Designs. Pale pink and brown is a combination popularized by old Hollywood and Art Deco design—it's Jean Harlow, 1920s glamour. Adding metallic accents, silver, gold, and gray solidify the movie-star atmosphere.

The designer Marlaina Teich, of Marlaina Teich Design, says, "Color has the power to change not only the look of your environment but also how you feel in it. Vibrant saturation can inspire and refresh. Soothing tones can relax and renew. You can set the mood by your choice of color." A perfect illustration is seen in the room pictured below. Swanky, chic, and shimmerlike, the distinctive and prized shade of Prussian blue has an aristocratic seventeenth-century French and English flair. Even today, this color looks expensive and deserving of its enduring rarified connotation. Touches of gold, silver, and glass set a sparkling stage fit for a queen.

SOFT, QUIET COLORS in the two rooms on this page are meant to be low key. These are private spaces where the homeowners go to be alone, concentrate, and relax.

Say What?

Colors can prattle, present a fluent and clearly defined message, or be hyper-expressive and even theatrical. Trying to categorize color is a fool's mission, but there exist distinctive combinations that will articulate a design agenda—therapeutic, for example, or a theme, such as air and sky.

hip and funky

Combinations categorized this way often feature colors that are not easily defined. A particular color may seem radical somehow because you can't quite figure out what it is at first glance. This type of color is often considered to be "on the cusp." In the general spectrum of all colors, this particular hue will actually fall between two distinct colors and reflect some characteristics of both of them. A good example would be any of the colors referred to as "not quite blue, not quite green."

Contrary by design, one wild-pattern drape installed as a deliberate departure from the mood of the space eliminates the seriousness of a formal look. I love a little guile, especially when it demands our attention like a foot-stomping teenager, which is why it always seems fresh and young. Assembling discordant colors in small accessories or details, such as wild and crazy patterns, takes some of the severity out of high-contrast modern color schemes. Use this ploy—it works every time.

While minimalist, well-edited, high-contrast palettes suggest modernity, particularly when they are in opposition to the overall feeling and design of a room. The inclusion of any singular unidentifiable cusp color turns modern into hip.

A cacophony of color on fabric, presented in abstract graphics or somewhat "mod" designs, always adds a hipster flair to a room as well. Vivid graphics displayed in conjunction with cusp colors hold nothing back but leave just a little to the imagination. Today, there is a retro connotation associated with orange, which is odd because the color has been widely available since long before the late-1960s-to-early-1970s era associated with it. Maybe it's all the Woodstock film footage. But orange is much more than a groovy color, and well worth a try. If solid orange isn't your bag, try it in a graphic pattern.

A MINIMALIST PALETTE looks modern in this home office, opposite. The scheme reinforces the room's clutter-free simplicity.

A MIX OF PATTERNS enlivens an almost all-neutral palatte, above. The blue, green, and brown curvy stripe of the table skirt's fabric makes the room look young and slightly less formal.

IT MAY BE FAR OUT, but this retro green shag stair runner with orange and pink fringe gives the vintage entry hall a hip-chic look.

down to earth

Yes, I love all things green, and no, I've never met a green I didn't love. As a color, nothing communicates outdoors, country, the familiar, and the natural quite like green. When a pleasing mid-range green is on the wall, it almost doesn't matter what else is in the room because it already feels pretty fine. But what happens when you step up the color, perhaps in a pairing?

No color answers to brown more clearly and concisely than green. Warm brown and bright or mid-range green combinations project a modern sensibility and begin a color conversation in an unexpected whisper. It is a combination that is so familiar outdoors that when you find yourself in its midst indoors you will immediately feel safe and well. Try it and see what happens.

AGAINST A DEEP BROWN BACK- GROUND, this room's green acces- sories and soft furnishings, above, left, and right, pop, visually bringing the outdoors inside this nature- inspired design. Touches of orange in the upholstered accent chair and some pillows, opposite top and bot- tom, add just enough contrast for interest.

A most lyrical depiction of a brown and green color scheme is illustrated on this and the opposite pages. "Some might shy away from using such a dark tone on a room's walls," says the designer, Kate Singer, of Kate Singer Home. "It can, however, provide a dramatic, cocoon–like setting for living."

She also says that you can keep this dramatic palette from looking or feeling dark using a few expert tricks.

"Cool metals and mirror tones on furniture pieces brighten the space as they reflect light. The geometric pattern on this room's rug, with its ivory background, provides a light and modern foundation for the space." Kate also suggests "keeping fabrics and furniture pieces lighter and brighter so they stand out and make a statement against the dark walls."

There are a few additional elements at work in this room worth considering for your own projects. The windows not only offer a relief and interruption in the wall color, but also provide a vista that ties the outside and inside together. The bark of the trees and the fall foliage or summer greens become one with the interior, and the entire space feels as though you are outdoors. It's also worth noting that each textile, from the green silk taffeta drape to the orange pillow, has a tactile reference to the leaves, bark, and grass.

The designer was perhaps too humble to explain her most cunning detail, the repetitive circles, which brings the form and reference of stones or pebbles to the design in the cream and bronze pillows, shimmery drapery detail, mirror, and lamp. Coming full circle, literally and figuratively, to the most understated reference in the room—the wall behind the sofa—begs the question, is that a mirror or is it the sun?

tweaking tradition

Color cards in hand, lighting and likes established, you can communicate your personality, style, and design point of view with the colors you choose. For example, this is a rather traditional kitchen as defined by the white painted cabinetry and the white marble counters.

The choice of marigold for the range is an enormous departure from traditional design dictums and brings an unconventional, and happy, surprise into the space. A predictable white tile backsplash does nothing to upset the peace, while the turquoise teapot continues the spirited color approach the marigold began. Vanilla-colored paint on the walls allows the colorful displays to set the mood and have all the fun.

Look at what happens when the vanilla wall color is accented by hues from a display of kitchen items that include cool icy aqua and luscious orange and green squash on the vine. It breaks up the large expanse of off-white with a palette of edible-referenced colors. This is how the cook's true personality is revealed, and these colorful references make the kitchen look and feel young, clean, well planned, and just plain delicious.

What about your own decorating challenge? Turn the page and find out how to make it work—with color!

appliance color

DO YOU DARE? Most people remember—with horror—the harvest gold appliances of yesterday. A trendy color can be risky. But, remember, you can refinish appliances today thanks to new paint products.

THE VANILLA WHITE is a far cry from the cool, crisp whites that can be too cold in a kitchen. It reflects natural light beautifully and offers an ideal canvas for colorful accessories that add personality-plus to the space.

CHAPTER 3

Architectural

play with color to alter the look and

Color
feel of physical space

What is meant by "architectural color?" For one thing, it is the use of color to **play up or play down** a room's architectural features. But color can also stand in for architectural **character** where there is little or none. It can connote a **style or period;** make a wall appear to recede or enclose a space more intimately; visually **reapportion space;** and bounce light into a room or absorb it almost entirely. Color may be the answer to **making over** a space without moving a wall or adding a window. Although some colors, by their very **strength,** seem to "feel" architectural, it is how you use them, alone or in combination, that makes **the difference.** Take a look.

AGAINST SLATE-BLUE-COLOR WALLS, this stone fireplace stands out as the focal point in the room. The creamy white on the trimwork and the ceiling is a welcome contrast to the deep, dark hue. Neutral tones on the upholstery, with just a few colorful accents, look earthy and comfortable.

Make It Work

The rooms in this chapter have something in common—their color schemes were carefully chosen to address particular architectural issues. Those "issues" were not necessarily defects or faults in the architecture. In fact, in many cases, color was key to enhancing the room's existing architecural features. However, you will find instances where color brought

architectural integrity

scaling the heights

from cookie-cutter to cutting edge

tall tales

character to a room where it was lacking. Other times, color played with a space to make visual adjustments to its proportions. But in every case, you'll see that the color scheme was conceived, foremost, to address the needs of the space in terms of its structure and not as an arbitrary decision based solely on preference and taste.

you + black and white

racing green

wall of color

call of the wild

Architectural Integrity

Color saves the day

Choosing a color scheme that is appropriate for a distinctive architectural style and yet modern can be tricky.

Here, a carefully chosen cadmium yellow is repeated in the artwork, fabrics, and other details. The blue adds vitality to the palette, without which the yellow would appear less bright or intense. The painted-black sashes and window muntins lend credibility to the color of the drapes, while the perimeter walls, large furnishings, and rug are all done in gray. By keeping the walls neutral, the design remains subtle and yet entirely glorious.

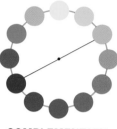

COMPLEMENTARY

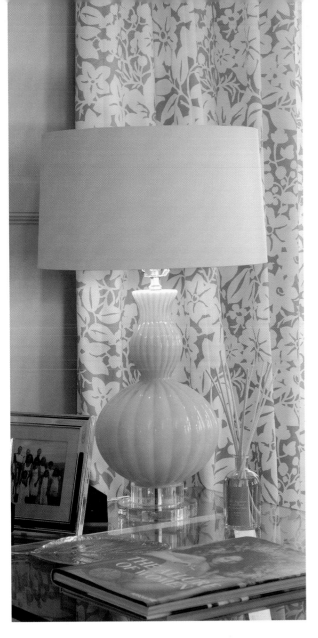

Dior Gray

Samoan Sun

New Black

Fountain Mist

design consult

"**I FOUND** I could say things with color and shapes that I couldn't say any other way," remarked artist Georgia O'Keeffe. That is a good way to consider the relationship between color and architecture, too. Color has more than decoration to offer a structure. There are times when it is the astute color scheme that makes the physical space work.

Laguna Blue

Amarillo

Hawthorne Yellow

Cream Yellow

MONOCHROMATIC

Scaling the Heights

Color saves the day

A mellow yellow and grayed-down green-blue visually alter the scale here, making this kitchen with a vaulted ceiling feel less cavernous and more personal.

Two-story-high rooms and vaulted ceilings can open up space—sometimes sacrificing what feels comfortable for what looks dramatic. But color can be a great equalizer, toning down architectural volume to a human level.

another option

IT WOULD BE NICE TO ADD BLUE to this palette because it is a color that works successfully with yellow. No matter how subtle and creamy the yellow may be, the addition of a grayed blue-green on the stools visually lifts the wall color. Keeping the blue-green choice rhythmic and subtle, the stools effortlessly settle into the black counter surface and the all-white perimeter. As a rule of thumb, kitchens that are generally well lit and large do not need overly saturated colors. So while this palette may seem a little understated at first glance, it actually suits the space perfectly.

North Sea Green

design consult

TONING THE YELLOWS and again using the same wall as an accent, a second, paler yellow could be added to the pitched ceiling. This puts a lot of color overhead, but it works as long as it is paler than the wall. (Add a little white to the wall color.) The toning keeps the overall effect from appearing jarring. It's interesting that the palette is completed with subtle accessories and, most surprisingly, by the green from the view. It is worth noting that were the same exact shade of yellow used on the ceiling and the wall, they would nevertheless still appear different in color, owing to the shadow each surface casts upon the other. Play this up, and you will keep the effect deliberate, and therefore, much more interesting.

a pinch of happy

WHETHER YOU LOVE THE COLOR OR NOT, small accents of orange are never wishy-washy or subtle. And research reveals that orange actually makes people feel happy. Accessories are perfectly suited for a dash of color, in this case, lively orange. If you haven't tried it, give it a chance. Orange can grow on you.

another option

WHILE I WHOLEHEARTEDLY AGREE with the selection of red as an accent to black and white, look at how transforming a different color can be and how it alters the mood.

Cut the Mustard

You + Black and White

Color saves the day

The high contrast of black and white exploits this room's strong, rustic architectural features, while keeping the overall look contemporary and refined.

Black lends modernity to a room, and nothing says "I hired an architect" more clearly than an all-white scheme. The designer of this room has combined the allure of classic elegance with an affable furniture arrangement that accentuates the warmth of the hearth and the friendly nature of the smaller design elements. The walls are not pure white, yet the room is still perceived as such, with the exception of a few colorful accents that soften the contrast. Adding a small amount of color, in this case red, personalizes the space and makes it look less decorated. A touch of glitz comes courtesy of the sunburst mirror over the mantel and antique-gold accents.

White Vanilla

New Black

Blushing Red

design consult

IN ORDER TO ACHIEVE THIS LOOK IN A LIVING SPACE, repeat the black at least three times. While I'm not one for rules in design, I like this one. If you are planning a room from scratch and can work in a few fabrics in varying textures that are solid black or black and white, count each one as a black in a white room. A lot is unnecessary, but it is helpful for the three uses of black to be on three different planes in the room.

Here is a fine example. The black and white draperies count as black number 1 in this white room. The back of the chairs, which are a fabulous black weave framed in solid black, is instance number 2. The third black, which solidifies the combination, is on the fireplace mantel, the beams overhead, the sofa legs, and the shades of the lamps. Presenting black number 3 on various horizontal, vertical, and floating planes completes this absolutely stunning look. The exploitation of high-contrast is a tried-and-true architectural device combination.

MAKE IT WORK • MAKE IT

Racing Green

Color saves the day

Some rooms, such as this bedroom, are plain white boxes devoid of any built-in interest or architectural detail. What's the easiest way to beat the architectural doldrums? Create line and form with color.

This racy, wide green stripe carves out an "architectural feature" where once there was merely a flat, white wall. Continuing the extra-wide stripe up and over the ceiling adds even more power to the statement. Kaboom!

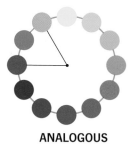

ANALOGOUS

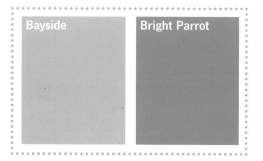

Bayside	Bright Parrot

other options

IN THIS VERSION, right, notice that the room falls flat without the dramatic green stripe, but is equally full of energy when a near cadmium yellow is substituted behind the bed, far right. This yellow is almost a pure primary and of equal weight, architecturally speaking, to the green, even though it has been softened with a drop of white. I think the room grew a little younger in feeling, but it is no less exhilarating thanks mostly to the blue-green lift from the bedding.

design consult

THE REMAINING COLORS IN THIS SCHEME don't scream, but deviate subtly from the brightness of the wall's palette. Low-key art pieces, an orange lamp, and understated black accents keep the color scheme moving, but not dizzying.

While there are a number of ways to present this palette in the room, the final results make the most of the owners' existing bedding and choice of a near black color for the flooring. The lamp looks awfully swell in a rather dramatic orange. If the bedding were that color, however, the overall mix could end up looking a little too much like a children's cartoon. Keeping the brightest color (orange) on the smallest piece (the lamp) and continuing to work through the combinations until the palest occupies the largest expanse of space (the white quilt) prevented the scheme from being too stimulating for the modest-size space.

Cliveden

Island Orange

Dark Kettle Black

From Cookie-Cutter to Cutting Edge

Color saves the day

Accentuating the line and volume of a typical hall in a Colonial-style tract house with an unusual progression of color adds vitality to the transitions from one space to another.

Voluminous entry foyers and open-plan great rooms are part of today's signature layouts, which suit a modern, informal lifestyle. Here, each color plays a part in personalizing the space and in moving the eye from one area to the next. The interior window, which pokes a hole through the orange, keeps the color and the hall from feeling dark. Reserving the darkest, strongest hue for the stairway landing is a logical, yet subtle, visual device that "grounds" the area.

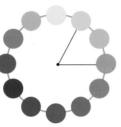

ANALOGOUS

Papaya	Rhumba Orange	Afternoon

design consult

BLOCKING SPACE IN CLOSELY RELATED COLORS that terminate in a white room or area is another example of how treating transitions using color can create excitement along the way. Framing the space beyond, right, with a complementary color (blue) is a simple decorative device that keeps the transition smooth, while more dramatic color choices seem to suggest you're on your way to a somewhere special.

Tall Tales

Color saves the day

Sometimes a room needs a little extra boost of color to make its proportions appear just right. Even soft furnishings, such as pillows or window treatments, can do the trick.

Expanding the palette by adding a touch more of the soothing blue gives this room a lift without disturbing the peace. Here's how: bringing the blue of the drapery band to the fitted pelmet above the panels immediately creates a sense of added height, drawing the eye up to the area just below the ceiling. Although the original design of the pelmet is architectural in concept, the white sat a little too quietly against the ethereal wall color. One more simple alteration to the plain lampshade enhances the blue effect and ties it into the trim of the drapery.

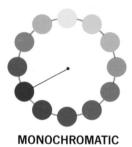

MONOCHROMATIC

| Celestial | Skier's Trail | Stylish Blue | Blue Flame | Geneva Blue |

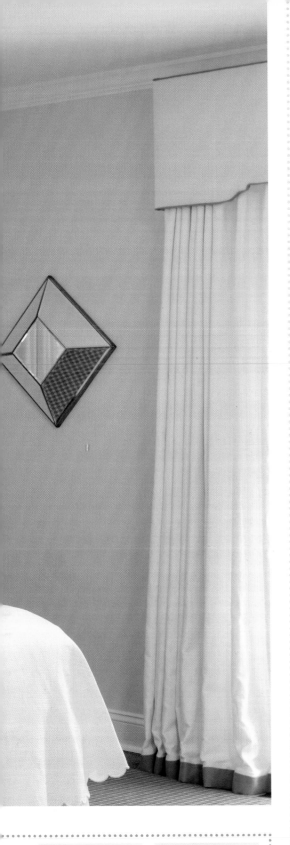

what can a humble lampshade say?

PLENTY. The color swatches, right, offer optional choices for the lampshade. Each one has characteristics that suggest something about the mood of the room and its occupant's personality. Remember, the color of your accessories can make a statement of their own.

New Black

BLACK
A little bit classic

Incense Stick

BROWN
Trendy and young

Fashion Gray

METALLIC
Glamourous

Geneva Blue

RICH BLUE
Let's go for a swim

Trieste Blue

Fountain Mist

MAKE IT WORK • MAKE IT WORK • MAKE IT WORK • MAKE IT WORK

Wall of Color

Color saves the day

Hawthorne Yellow	Cherry Tomato	Jersey Cream

The openness of loft living can be appealing, but it presents a challenge when you want to define an area or create a partition without completely closing off a space.

The solution? Color blocking a wall to create an architectural focal point. It will have the strength to stand on its own if the color is powerful. Try to go as strong in your color choice as the space and your sensibilities can abide. Freestanding blocks of color are less successful if the color appears tentative; go for the gusto, as this beautifully conceived tomato red example demonstrates. This wall stands in the middle of a rather long expanse of loft space, and it figuratively and literally suggests that there is something exciting happening on the other side of it. (It's the kitchen!)

ANALOGOUS

THE RED WALL is a good choice for a dining room, left. See how it defines an area in this loft while keeping the public spaces open to one another, opposite, bottom.

another option

COLOR BLOCKING will lend depth to a room when viewed from a distance if you use a cool hue. Alternately, painting the wall a warm color will make a room more intimate. Notice what happens when cool blue-green replaces the red, right. Whereas red is stimulating, blue and green are "slow down and relax" colors that are better suited for private, rather than public areas in the home. The color here is a little too serious for a place meant for socializing.

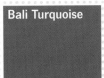

Bali Turquoise

Call of the Wild

Color saves the day

Making use of a small space under the stairs is a smart idea, and this wild black and white zebra motif makes something special out of a nook. Now laundry day is almost exciting!

Not for the faint of heart, this spine-tingling scheme is an artistic tour de force that makes a big deal out of a tiny space. The simplicity of the black and white in concert with the oversize all-over pattern creates a lively vibe in the "room." The black-and-white combination fits right in with the typically bold colors of laundry doings, and while I have not personally had the pleasure of spending time drying and folding in this amusing little space, I imagine that laundry day moves along as swiftly as a safari.

New Black

Ultra White

go for it

DO YOU HEAR HOOFBEATS?
Never overlook the chance to exploit an architectural feature. I think of slanted ceilings and complicated little spaces as opportunities for adding unexpected energy or even humor to an unusual space. When you're faced with one of these situations, go ahead: add an exhuberant color or pattern.

a coloful slant

CALLING ATTENTION to slanted walls or ceilings with dramatic color can turn an eyesore into an invigorating room feature. The brightest sunny yellow is as pleasing as the morning sun in the room below. Keep in mind that a yellow that is this intense is known to make people nervous, and it can be hard on the eyes. But if you use it with restraint, the color's reflective value can brighten a dead corner. Because the slant of the wall softens the reflected daylight that bathes this south-facing room, it is both successful and wild.

Imperial Yellow

COLOR MAKES THE MOST out of this dark corner under the roof. The bright hue perks up the mood of the space. Now, instead of feeling gloomy, the guest room is a cheerful, welcoming retreat. This is a good example of how a light or bright color visually "lifts" a wall or ceiling.

Accentuate Great Features

Color saves the day

Sheer draperies in bold red accentuate a bank of windows and a dramatically high ceiling in this otherwise all-white-and-wood scheme.

Facing west to the mountains, just imagine how this color scheme collaborates with the view in autumn. Every evening, the colors of the pillows complement the exciting hues of sunset.

ANALOGOUS

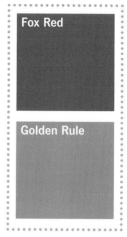

Fox Red

Golden Rule

another option

THIS ROOM IS EQUALLY GORGEOUS WITH LAVENDER BLUE SHEERS, which would be a good choice if the space faced east. Eastern morning light is cooler than that of a warmer western exposure. This is a great example of how fostering a relationship between the inside and the outside through the use of color solidifies the personality of a room and the effectiveness of the colors. While I could play all day with other enchanting combinations, in the end, the designer selected the perfect color to enhance the warmth of the breathtaking Nevada sky.

Blue Viola

DRAPERIES THAT REACH THE CEILING and raise the eye do more than visually elevate a room. Here, the art can also go vertical because the tall bay window balances the arrangement. Bouncing the rich porcelain blue along the sofa and up the drapery band creates a lively color scheme without the room appearing simply blue. It's the vitality of the blue, which has several classic references and Eastern influences, that is creating the sense of European opulence in the room.

CHAPTER 4

Color
update your home inexpensively

for Now
with fresh "now" colors

Thoreau said, "Simplify, simplify, simplify." Maybe everyone had more time to dust the furniture and more money to invest in goofy accessories a few years ago, but now there is a movement underway to conserve more and consume less. And while the desire for more media equipment hasn't waned, the amount of space required to house all of it is shrinking every day. People are downsizing. However, creating a well-edited look that is still comfortable and pleasing is more difficult than it seems. You'll need to send the dried flowers over to grandma's, and start looking for ways to jack up the simplest and most cost-effective design tool you have—color.

ACCESSORIES introduce appealing new color to this almost-all-white kitchen. The somewhat unconventional choice (for a kitchen) of violet and green puts a contemporary spin on the traditional architecture.

Make It Work

Updating your home with the latest colors is sure to keep your home looking stylishly chic. In this chapter, you'll find palettes that are all the rage at the moment. Just remember, color for the home can fall victim to trends. While you can ride out a craze or pass on what may be nothing more than a fleeting fad, some trends are sensible developments

luxe hotel living

beyond basic

rethink pink

calling all neutrals

worthy of exploration. If you're not interested in going on a long ride or making a big change, there are a number of effective colors and dream designs that don't require starting from scratch to achieve—and the investment of time and money is minimal. Better yet, you can make changes easily when, once again, you're looking for something new.

modern times

hit the refesh button

adding personality with stripes

today's color news

Luxe Hotel Living

Color saves the day

Some people loved to be pampered. This bedroom's new palette makes it feel like an upscale getaway, even though it's at home.

Black furniture and accessories look urbane and lend the feeling of a boutique hotel that "staycationers" will appreciate. In a bedroom, there are only few wall colors that don't look fabulous accented with black (only purple comes to mind). Blue is a particularly good companion color for black, and the addition of a little sparkle and a small kick of white looks clean and peacefully spare.

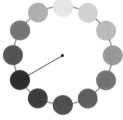

MONOCHROMATIC

Arctic Blue

Bone Black

Almafi Navy

another option

SWITCH THE WALL COLOR and change this room from peaceful to cozy with an earthy light brown. Try this if the room gets cool northern light. But be careful not to go too dark with a brown in any room that gets little natural light.

Ivoire

design consult

TAMING UNRULY BLUES Cool blues are what I call bossy colors—they like to run the show. Because so many blues like to dominate the color conversation and need to stand alone, mixing them with black is a sure way to make them behave.

Blues that lean a little toward the green or aqua range, or periwinkle as well as the lavender blues, have the complexity to balance plenty of black and look up to the minute—dare I say, trendy—doing so. Cool, gray, watery blues are more easily mixed and matched and are equally terrific companions to black.

Honolulu	Chi	Angora Blue	Watercolor Blue	Surf's Up	Ocean Breeze

Beyond Basic

Color saves the day

Black works magic, once again. This time in a dining room that needed an accent, but not necessarily one with color.

While I hate to usurp the designer's beautiful work, I am obliged to point out that this stunning look could be achieved with just about any table and chairs made black. For example, you could refinish an old Parsons table from the 1970s in an espresso color to easily update the look. Here, leather chairs and other black accents, such as the black picture frames and drapery rod, complete the design picture.

The simple, understated line of the drapery rod keeps the black of the table and chairs from creating a dark mood in the room. The white drapes provide a backdrop for the depth of the black, and the art is another expression of the subtle design. The rhythmic silver vases that "push" the black around are brilliant in more ways than one.

Black Truffles	Edwardian Linen

design consult

EXTRA SPECIAL For the budget-conscious, it's handy to know that you can give any assortment of mismatched or old furniture pieces a "now" look with an espresso-toned glaze and a tinted polyurethane finish. Make sure you sand and clean the pieces properly, and apply a flat black latex base coat. Then, using a good-quality brush, go over the furniture with a dark brown oil glaze, consisting of equal parts of raw umber, burnt umber, and burnt sienna universal tints. Let it dry. Two coats of polyurethane, tinted the same color as the glaze, will provide a durable protective finish.

A SIDE TABLE with an espresso finish mixes easily with other dark woods. Colorful orange-red art and flowers accent this rich hue beautifully.

Modern Times

Color saves the day

Once again, oh what a little black can do to update a permanent feature in a room that you thought you could not change. Case in point—a dated paneled wall in a dining room suited a previous owner's style, but it didn't work for the most-recent residents' modern sensibilities. Painting one wall black and the rest of the paneling white brightens the space. A new light fixture and abstract art make it chic, sophisticated, and contemporary.

If you would like to take a sledgehammer to an ugly or obtrusive permanent feature in your house, but you can't, chances are it will look much less obvious painted black. And like the wall in this room, it may actually become a stunning design element.

fireplace 911

THE FIREPLACE below is actually 6 x 9 feet of brick from floor to ceiling in the room, and it continues through to the top of the house. I concealed and covered it with all of the drywall the fire codes would allow and outfitted it with a rustic mantel, and it still looked ugly. Happily, a can of high-heat black paint solved that problem before lunch (left).

A VINTAGE WINDOW with mirrored glass and black-painted muntins reflects the black-paneled wall from the opposite side of the room.

Black Truffles

Lacey Pearl

design consult

AS SOPHISTICATED AND VERSATILE AS A LITTLE BLACK DRESS you can wear anywhere, a little black paint looks swanky on just about anything. Every good room deserves a little black somewhere, and even a little bit is a go-everywhere, do-everything, always smart-looking affair. Black makes quick work of old doors, window sashes, picture frames, and odd furniture pieces. Don't underestimate the power of black to add a modern or classic sensibility to just about any spot in the house. Even lampshades look smart decked out in black.

Cork

Whipple Blue

BEFORE

Hit the Refresh Button

Color saves the day

To wake up this lovely slice of Americana without giving it a complete makeover, I changed the wall color from a tired, pale creamy ochre to a rich golden ochre. This highly saturated, complex color provides a strong background for the fireplace and looks dazzling behind the white chairs. While simply adding a brick- or cinnabar-color pillow would add a nice touch to the space, it would not be enough to liven things up without the new wall color.

COMPLEMENTARY

Nearly the color of pure ochre pigment but somehow greener, redder, grayer, and browner, it is a brassy gold that is, as they say in the paint business, a good color because it is ambiguous, versatile, not clean, not dirty, not bright, not dull, not hot, not cool. It's not neutral, either, but it's pretty darn close.

design consult

NOW THAT THE WALLS ARE WHISTLING A HAPPY TUNE, you can turn your paintbrush loose on the trim. A red that lives somewhere between orange and burgundy would be nice, but I think the very discernable honesty of the blue, which has a good bit of red, adds some heritage to the room. It also keeps the transformation a little different and somewhat more refined.

Colorado Rust

Finally, add the cinnabar pillow, which could be a duller, blacker cherry red or an orange-brick iron oxide kind of red. Lest our red, white, and blue scheme appear too literal, it's probably best letting the red be as ambiguous as the gold.

Cinco de Mayo

Lady Pink

Snowfield

Veil

Dover Grey

Rethink Pink

Color saves the day

Paint walls pink in a room shared by a male and a female? Yes, it's doable, but pink needs a masculine influence, or it takes over and looks too "girlie." What makes this room sophisticated and less gender-specific is the addition of gray to the scheme.

The vase, the rug, the bleached floor, the drapery rod, even some of the brick on the fireplace—all read gray in this room. By adding gray or black to a pink palette such as this, you cancel out the "for young girls or grannies only" impression because people perceive gray as a masculine color. However, gray can be a very chic color, as well. Think of those classic gray tweed suits. In addition gray has a somewhat serious personality, which can tone down some of pink's perkiness. This combination of colors is truly a balancing act between a hue that is always cheerful, sometimes even whimsical, and one that can be gentle but not feminine.

MONOCHROMATIC

other options

THE MORE GRAY YOU ADD, the less feminine the room becomes. Take a look at what gray curtains do for the overall scheme. Then look at what happens when you make the chair gray, too.

If you like a more saturated, flamboyant pink, pair it with a deeper shade of gray—one that is of equal value.

design consult

PINK AND GRAY are the best example of this feminine versus masculine, yin/yang thing because they balance each other. Think about a man in a pink shirt; he looks fine if he's in a black or gray suit, but not so much if he's wearing white linen pants. Same thing is happening here. (Sure, it's a matter of personal taste, but I think most people would agree.) Black would have a similar effect, but gray is more understated, and therefore, sophisticated.

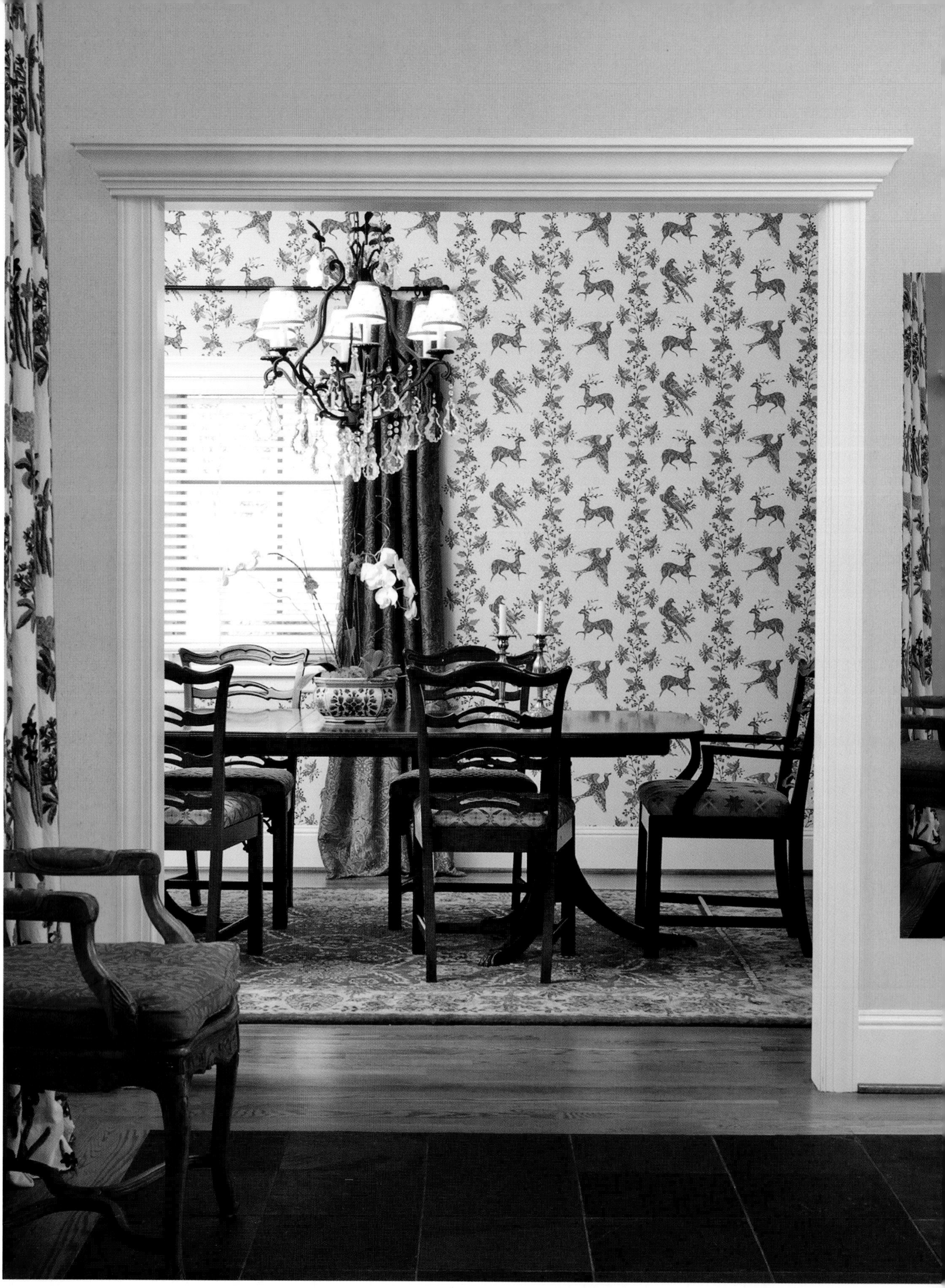

Calling All Neutrals

Color saves the day

BEFORE

A traditional, well-dressed dining room was not served well by an adjacent yellow hall. Exchanging the yellow for gray, however, reduced the contrast between the two spaces making the dining room's red more deliberate and the wallcovering's pattern more apparent. This is the essence of "now" design—surrounding good color choices that can stand on their own or with a harmonious chorus.

Painting the hall gray warmed by red undertones creates an effortless transition for this space. The gray looks clean surrounded by the white trim, and the red in the wallpaper is reaping every reward a neutral foreground can provide—it looks brighter, richer, more complex, and most importantly, of the moment. The flooring, upholstery, and wood tones all harmonize with the gray, forming one unanimous collection of neutrals that supports the red and allows it to sing. Ta-da!

MONOCHROMATIC

design consult

OH NO, YOU DIDN'T I really hate it when design professionals deem a color to be "neutral," when what I think they mean to say is they feel neutral about the color. This is the story of the most ambiguous, delightful, friendly, color you can choose, yellow. Yellow is not, repeat not, a neutral color. In fact, it is a primary color, and there is nothing neutral about it. Now that I have that out of my system, let me add that it's a useful, safe, and obliging color because, by and large, everyone feels just plain all right about it, especially its pale versions. The only thing bad you'll ever hear anyone say about yellow is, "I'm so tired of it." Personally, I feel the same about yellow as I do about a 4-year-old—seemingly obliging, well behaved, and sweet, but it can and will get on your nerves after a while. When you finally wish it to be gone, it simply has got to go.

Blushing Red

Stone Harbor

Coastal Fog

Mesa Verde Tan

Taos Taupe

Silver Fox

Abalone

MAKE IT WORK • MAKE IT WORK • MAKE IT WORK

Stroke of Genius

Color saves the day

We've all been there. You paint a room, but the new color just isn't working. Adding a dynamic faux finish or paint technique over the base you've just created may be the answer. This bronze glaze softened a bright, gold wall color.

Not a single color can warm up a wall surface in the same way as a glazing technique. Transparent glaze colors can be applied over clean and sound walls, which are painted an understated or neutral color. Here, the mood of the glossy golden glaze adds a depth and interest to the walls, calls attention to the singular gold pillow, and accents the sofa. The look is simple but not severe.

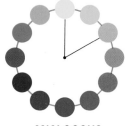

ANALOGOUS

how to mix a perfect glaze

There are different formulas with various advantages and disadvantages, depending on the technique you wish to apply to a wall. However, here are two basic general-purpose formulas.

- For an alkyd (oil-based) glaze, mix: 4 parts glazing liquid, 4 parts solvent, colorant.*
- For a latex (water-based) glaze, mix: 4 parts glazing liquid, 2 parts water, colorant.*

*Universal tints are colorants that mix easily with any type of paint. Other colorants include, but are not limited to, Japan paint, milk paint, and enamel.

Before attempting this type of project, consult one of the many fine books that explain the process. Then practice on a board until you get the look you wish to achieve. Your other option is to hire a professional who specializes in decorative paint techniques.

design consult

OFF-THE-SHELF PROPRIETARY
GLAZING LIQUIDS include both
alkyd (oil-based) and latex (water-
based) formulations. There are
several differences between them,
chiefly the drying time.

An alternative to a glaze is a wash,
which is simply thinned latex paint.
Colors that are too vibrant or just
plain ugly can be toned down or
changed quickly and dramatically
with a wash. A basic wash is simply
latex paint thinned with water.

Glitzy Gold

Relic Bronze

Artist Brown

Chesapeake Sunset
Pocket Watch White
Hunter Orange

Adding Personality with Stripes

Color saves the day

A basement usually doesn't offer a lot of character unless you add it, which is what happened in this family room with a personality-plus paint job. Because there is no natural light in the space, the owners chose a happy palette of orange and yellow. Wide stripes painted in bold yellow and white lighten the mood and provide a reflective surface for the artificial light sources.

Painted stripes are a popular way to add color today, and they are not difficult. However, you must measure—and mask—your walls carefully, choosing a width that works the best for you. You can cheat if need be, adjusting the width at small intervals so that you end at each corner with a full stripe.

ANALOGOUS

design consult

THERE ARE A LOT OF WAYS TO PLAY WITH COLOR when you are painting stripes or blocks on a wall. Tone-on-tone treatments look particularly sophisticated. You can do this by using two shades of the same color or by alternating the sheen (going from matte to gloss) with every other stripe. For a modern look, paint horizontal stripes. For expert results, apply a lighter "scumble glaze" (4 parts glazing liquid and 6 parts solvent or water) over the striped or color-blocked wall once it is completely dry. It will level out the sheen and add depth while diffusing the edges ever so slightly.

another option

HERE'S A STRIPE that doesn't need measuring or taping if you have a good eye. Try out your color on a sample board. Here, the warm medium tone of cornflower blue, similar to that of the headboard, contrasts with the existing pale wall and puts some oomph into the background. The cool blue and wiggle of the stripe also adds movement to the space and functions as art.

Bed of Roses	**Stratosphere**

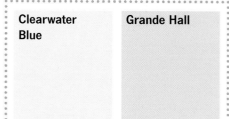

Clearwater Blue

Grande Hall

BEFORE

BEFORE

Swiss Almond

Desert Sand

Today's Color News

Color saves the day

In a contemporary layout where public spaces are open to one another, a coordinated or similar color scheme is important. But different colors were easy to pull off here because they share common traits.

Here are three rooms on the same floor of the same house. Each room has its own signature color, but all three work beautifully together. They have been updated in a muted, of-the-moment palette that looks deceptively neutral but actually goes from blue to brown to green. Using the same value of each color in a grayed-down version is a trick to making the overall look cohesive and modern.

Spider's Web   Grey Nuance

BEFORE

CHAPTER 5

Extreme

as an overall palette or in

Color
small doses, it's extremely spectacular

The language of extreme color is as **deliberate and precise** as the colors it describes: cobalt blue, chartreuse green, chrome yellow, and crimson red. These hues are **not for a shy or tentative** color picker who tends to open the fan deck just **far enough** to see the selections on top. In fact, I call the few clients I run across who **really love extreme color** my "bottom of the deckers." But there is a place in every home for these intense, **saturated, and precise** colors, once you have a fix on how and where to use them to further your **design aspirations.** As you'll see here, some extreme-color **statements are large** while others are small—but powerful.

AN OVER-THE-TOP COLOR SCHEME of vivid pinks and greens throws color caution to the wind. The playful palette lightens the mood of the room's formal architecture. Fuzzy carpet tiles were used to extend the fun underfoot.

Make It Work

Definitive high-impact colors will reveal your sense of adventure and add some pizzazz to less-than-jazzy places. As you'll see in some of the following examples, there doesn't have to be a lot of the color, but it does have to be extreme. In other instances, you may be surprised to see how one strong color can pull together an entire room—even if it has been

added zest

warm it up with yellow

orange crush

tart and tasty

furnished with a collection of different styles or mismatched pieces. Above all, you'll discover that because these homeowners refused to play it safe, the results have paid off in rooms that are loaded with personality and extraordinary design. Turn the page and see how color—extreme color—saves the day in rooms that needed a big, bold, boost.

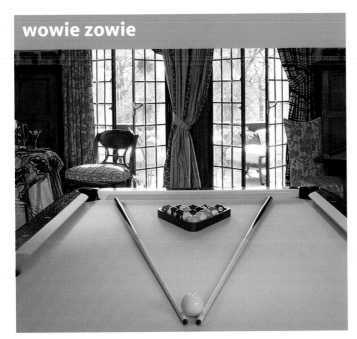

wowie zowie

the pink sofa in the room

blue haven

true blues

primary colors

Added Zest

Color saves the day

In this kitchen, orange was voted the family's most-desired accent color. The chairs add a lot of vitality to the open kitchen-and-dining-room combination, and the fantastic chandelier has the same fun-loving disposition as the orange.

Because the walls are painted in the happiest shade of pure, unadulterated yellow, there are numbers of audacious options for a singular, sensational color accent. Let's explore a few.

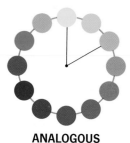

Crowne Hill
Yellow

Mesa Sunrise

ANALOGOUS

other options

**Frosted
Pomegranate**

THE CRIMSON is just as divine with the vivid, cool yellow. It is the intensity of the colors that is really exploiting this classic combination and keeping the overall effect modern. The luscious green trees beyond will add another dimension to the palette throughout the spring and summer—green is the complement to red. The yellow color on the walls has no green in it, however, which is why the contrast is striking and deliberate.

**California
Dreaming**

LIKE THE ORIGINAL orange selection, green is analogous to the yellow, making it an equally sound choice. Considering the view, it may be too much green, but the choice is compelling all the same. This particular green has a good deal of yellow in it, which has been mixed with a cerulean blue. Let's see what happens when you add a little blue to the mix, below.

Winter Surf

HERE'S AN EXAMPLE of how keeping an open mind when choosing a wall color can make a room come together so beautifully that it's hard to make a mistake. The clarity of the yellow is keeping it nearly neutral, and now the chairs look hip, metropolitan, and viridian. I like this combination—it's as crisp and vibrant as the orange and yellow.

Warm Up with Yellow

Color **saves the day**

In a rather long living room with distinctive features—large windows, an imposing traditional fireplace, and handsome trimwork—a rich and vivid yellow is perfect. This particular shade of yellow has the strength to support the elaborate architecture while it ensconces the room with a warm glow.

Yellow in the living room is a classic choice, but choosing the right one can be tricky. With the exception of the green-yellows, extreme yellow looks good with any number of equally saturated accent colors.

design consult

THERE ARE SOME SPACES where the sun is unpredictable. One instance is a west-facing room with windows that capture afternoon sun filtered through a few trees. Bright yellows with green in them will look vibrant in these rooms. Unlike the cool light of a northern orientation, the western sunlight is warmed by red, lavender, and pink. Choosing the sharper, greenish yellows will cool the space.

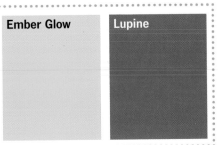

Ember Glow | Lupine

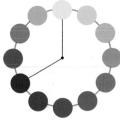

PRIMARY

another option

A COOLER SHADE OF YELLOW is equally lovely, but it lacks the guts to balance the high-contrast scheme that includes an intense blue. Furthermore, it does not provide enough "structure" for the architectural elements. This is a good example of how using an extremely saturated color not only defines the palette but also advances the design mandate.

Sunburst

vivid yellows

WHILE I CALL THIS CHROME or cadmium yellow, it's in fact a yellow produced by your paint manufacturer with modern synthetic pigments that are lightfast and opaque. Were you to mix the color yourself, natural cadmium yellow pigment and white would produce this clear and brilliant hue. The good news is that there's not a trace of green in either mixture, keeping the color intense and warm. For paler yellows that are equally clear, choose a shade that has just a whisper of orange in it.

Wowie Zowie

Color saves the day

Using extreme color, this homeowner was willing to go all out—way, way outside the box—to turn a somewhat stuffy room into a fun space for playing pool and partying. The bright pink-and-green palette instantly tones down the anything but playful look of the architecture.

The room is stately, with rich paneling, high ceilings, an imposing stone fireplace, and tall French doors leading to a formal terrace. But the uninhibited and whimsical color scheme of hot pink and tangy green looks young and modern, banishing any sense of reserve.

Bright Lime

Silk Ribbon

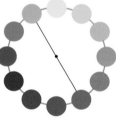

COMPLEMENTARY

INDIVIDUAL PINK AND GREEN CARPET rounds under and around the pool table provide a fun alternative to a traditional rug. The colors pop against the dark-stained wood floor.

RACK THEM UP. Bright pink felt puts an extreme color spin on the pool table top.

design consult

CHUMP CHANGE? Not here. Although another home may be more modest in scale, the point remains the same—color can transform the personality of a space entirely. When it is extreme color, it can overcome even the strongest architectural features, making a formal space look and feel more casual; take years off the looks of an old house; or add the appearance of age to a new home in need of character or historic reference.

The Pink Sofa in the Room

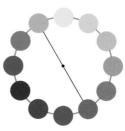

COMPLEMENTARY

Color saves the day

The owners of this more modest older home fell in love with a vintage sofa upholstered in pink velvet. Like brown and orange, pink is a love-it-or-hate-it kind of color—especially in the living room. Happily, these homeowners made an appealing case for it by adding olive green to the mix.

Olive—a slightly dirty, complex green—is a color the paint industry and design professionals label "drab." This is a green that may or may not have an authentic period heritage, but it suggests age, appearing a little weathered and a little grayed. Together, the two colors form a remarkable study in contrast and subtlety that few similar combinations ever inspire.

Henderson
Buff

Silk Ribbon

Livingston
Gold

Foxy Pink

LIKE PINK AND GREEN, PINK AND YELLOW is a color story that never seems to get tired. Yellows are not generally described as cool, but the green-yellows and the sharp, clear, cadmium yellows shimmer in a sunny room.

design consult

THE PINKS in this period room, opposite, run the shade and tone gamut from end to end, but the striking and slightly irides-cent intensity of the luminous draperies does nothing to upset the slightly magenta velvet on the old sofa. From the soft coral porcelain shades all the way to the screaming magentas, pink is a color that looks stunning when it is bathed in sunshine. It will brighten up a dark room with equal reliability, as well. Pink has a longstanding and historically significant relationship with nearly every green that exists—a good thing because green does not hold up well alone in bright sunlight or in deep shade.

WHEN THE PINK IS TOWARD THE HOTTER MAGENTA RANGE, very little of it is needed to provide a perfect complement to an all-yellow room. English Chintz and palettes derived from powerful French pink and green color stories are classically romantic and exceedingly pretty.

MAKE IT WORK • MAKE IT WORK • MAKE IT WORK

Orange Crush

Color saves the day

An orange rug, draperies, and accessories weren't enough for this homeowner, who felt the room wasn't coming together. A lover of orange, she felt she wasn't using the color to its best effect. The solution was applying a toned orange to the ceiling. As this homeowner learned, sometimes more is not less, after all.

Orange is not an easy color to make work. Here, applying a toned-down version of the color actually minimizes the jolt orange has the habit of delivering. There is a lot of artificial lighting in this room, which is adding an extra dose of warmth to the already bright space and color. The singular black lampshade and fushia pillows create the needed contrast and punctuate the color scheme.

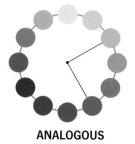

ANALOGOUS

design consult

ON THE COLOR WHEEL, orange lives somewhere between red—the more organic, warm, "burnt" side of the color—and yellow, its playful, childlike side. If you choose to do a room in orange, follow the lead of this clever designer, and go all the way.

More notable is the absence of colors that do not and could not occupy the space. This is a magical room, which I'm guessing elicits an excited gasp from all who are lucky enough to spend time in it. Itinerant red slippers or oddball accessories would wreak havoc on the well-planned and carefully conceived design, which is why even devout followers of orange, like me, look longingly upon such a fabulous space with envy, fan deck and fabrics in hand.

EARTHY, REDDISH ORANGES tempered with softer coral shades look beautiful with their complement blue—any blue.

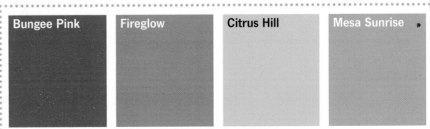

| Bungee Pink | Fireglow | Citrus Hill | Mesa Sunrise |

Tart and Tasty

Color saves the day

This homeowner was afraid to use a bright color in her sunny kitchen. Sun-loving, side-by-side greens changed her mind.

The kitchen is bathed in light from sunup to sundown. The acid green is clear and bright, and the cobalt blue accents add a luminous quality to the sharp yellow-green hue. A large grid pattern allows for the addition of a warm winter white, which makes the room feel a little cozier at night and when the snow arrives.

Fresh Cut
Grass

Apple Green

Honorable
Blue

design consult

TAKE THE PLUNGE in rooms and places around the house that are better suited to absorb the impact of an extreme wall color or an extreme combination of hues. In a sunny space that gets a lot of natural light, vivid colors that are considered sharp or even brilliant can hold their own. Pure colors are nearly devoid of white, which would soften them. They remain honest, uncomplicated, technically simple, and true to the pigment from which they are made. These are the vernacular colors, and they all love the sun.

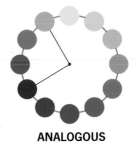

ANALOGOUS

another option

HERE'S THE SAME ROOM in a similar but more biting lime green. The color is less yellow now, and so it becomes very sharp. It is a synthetic color and cannot be produced using natural pigments. This choice works best in a hot climate, particularly if the view is overlooking the back nine.

Bright Lime

Yew Green

New Lime

MAKE IT WORK • MAKE IT WORK • MAKE IT WORK

Blue Haven

$Color$ saves the day

A large pattern can be just as daring as one solid, extreme color—maybe more so. In a spare bedroom that is sparsely furnished, bold color and pattern make up for what's missing with personality plus.

The background in this cheery wallcovering is an ultramarine-derived blue. The color is supporting a complex analogous palette that spans nearly the entire cool side of the color wheel in a masterful and harmonious symphony of variations. Few other colors could pull off this feat without creating a discordant result.

ANALOGOUS

another option

IF A COLORFUL, LARGE-PRINT WALLCOVERING is too over the top for your taste, go for broke with a dramatic paint color—which is easier to change—and save the print for the fabrics or an upholstered piece.

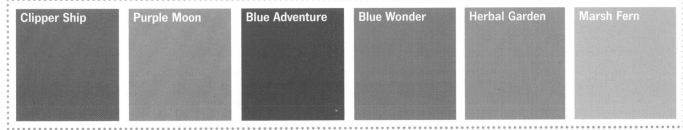

Clipper Ship	Purple Moon	Blue Adventure	Blue Wonder	Herbal Garden	Marsh Fern

design consult

IT IS A DANGEROUS GAME to blithely assemble more than five adjoining colors on the color wheel. The only reason why this seemingly carefree collection works is that there is only one primary in the bunch—blue. It's tricky, and if either of the next colors (yellow or red) on the color wheel were added to the mix, the result would be a mess!

MAKE IT WORK • MAKE IT WORK • MAKE IT WORK

True Blues

Color saves the day

Bedrooms and baths that get more than their share of sun are stunning in luxurious blues. Gray-blues, especially those with red or purple undertones, look cold and washed out in sunny rooms and are better suited to a northern exposure.

Blue is popular in bedrooms, and this one is no exception. Keeping the blue clear and well defined absorbs the light of the day and stays true to its cheerful side.

Blues that have absolutely not a speck of green in them, and are faithful to the ultramarine tint from which they are derived, can be used on large expanses of wall without appearing overwhelming. These are pure blues, which work well with other shades of blue, as well as with the colors green and lavender.

Frank Blue

Crisp Linen

design consult

AN EXTREMELY ENERGETIC palette of blue, black, yellow, and red is something everyone has seen in the art of Calder, Miro, and Mondrian. It is surprisingly easy to live with the collection in any room in the house, and it can be expanded upon or simplified to work to your taste.

Because the combination is so familiar, tweaking even a single one of the colors, in this case replacing the primary cobalt blue with a softer aqua, for example, would result in an entirely different feeling in the room. Fiddling a little more with the primary blue, moving the red toward brick, reducing the black, and keeping the brightest color—the lemon yellow—nearly absent would transform this modern color collaboration into an eclectic classic.

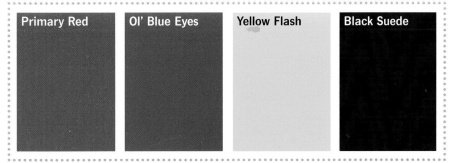

| Primary Red | Ol' Blue Eyes | Yellow Flash | Black Suede |

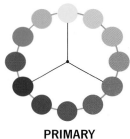

PRIMARY

AN ALL-PRIMARY PALETTE, which was inspired by the painting, enhances the modern look of this room.

CHAPTER 6

For the

have it your way, all-white or

Color-Shy

simply subtle and sensational

Limiting a room to white or any single color can be more complicated than it seems. And let's face it, a monochromatic palette does not take into account what you will do with Aunt Millie's crocheted blanket or your collection of vintage pink-and-green table linens. Often, people who claim to be shy about color are really not afraid of it at all. In truth, they are afraid of paint colors. If you get weak in the knees standing at a color-chip display, not to worry: there are plenty of extraordinary ways to introduce a little color into your home, sometimes without ever having to open a can of paint. And if you still want to stick with white, here's what you should know.

A VARIETY OF COMPATIBLE WHITES come together in this subtle palette that was designed as a backdrop to a view of the sea.

Whites by Design

There is, for sure, a difference between choosing to live in a harmonious, colorless surrounding of pure white and arriving in such a circumstance by default. All-white schemes are often impressive, particularly when some planning and effort is made to keep them that way. White is not considered a color. If you have no affinity for color whatsoever, then an all-white palette is a logical choice.

Choosing the Right White

White comes in all sorts of shades and tones, and there are countless variables in each one. Creamy whites have just a tinge of yellow. The ones referred to as "French Whites" have cool, silvery undertones and are generally what you see on white drapery or lampshades. There are white paint colors with names, such as "Picket Fence," "Parchment," "Ivory," "China White," "Pearl White," "White Dove," and "Pale Bloom," to name a few. In the absence of another white for comparison, any one of them will look like just plain white—even to a well-trained eye.

Fine artists rely on a more technical vocabulary when speaking of whites—namely titanium, zinc, and flake whites.

However, artists rarely use any white as delivered. Instead, they mellow it by adding raw umber or black tint, causing the white to gray; tint it using a little yellow ochre to create a warm, buttery undertone; or brighten it by mixing a miniscule amount of blue into it. (So-called "Ceiling White," "Decorator White," or "Super White," are all proprietary paint formulas that contain some amount of blue.) Artists also make pinkish whites using reds, delicate whites with lilac undertones using purple, and on it goes.

When you are choosing your white, whether for a ceiling, wall, or trim application, be sure to compare each varying shade the manufacturer of your choice provides. Take the time to do a test swatch on a wall in the room you will paint. Keep in mind that all manner of white materials, including carpets and all fabrics, will each be their own representation. In fact, some bath-fixture manufacturers offer no less than four variations of white; the difference between each one is nearly imperceptible. With some practice, you will be able to discern between a crisp, cool one and something warm and glowing. Let the room's lighting and furnishings help guide your choice. Remember, design fortune is on your side when a good mixture of warm and cool whites are incorporated into a space.

Gypsum	Glazed Pears
Heirlom Lace	Witch Hazel
Horseradish	Peach Linen

SOME WHITES are cool (left); others are warm (right). A white room with a northern exposure will look slightly blue, while a space with a southern or a western exposure will reflect a purer white.

Warm Yellow Whites

design consult

WARM YELLOW WHITES make lovely wall colors. If your style is vintage, but your house is brand new, these whites will imply a little age. Use them for trim details with warm beiges and blues, as well as with yellow, gold, and red.

Featherstone	Linen White	White Beacon	Llama White
Navajo White	Adobe White	Milk Paint	Cameo White

design consult

NEARLY BLUE WHITES are fantastic on a ceiling. Any one of them is a good companion color for the entire gray range. Especially pleasing with warm pinks and all greens except lime or chartreuse, these are the whites to use in bright homes or in rooms with less-than-perfect exposures that you would like to brighten. Blue whites mix well with other whites. I have a personal fascination for using them with deeply saturated colors

Cool Blue Whites

Silent Delight

Moonlit Snow

White Dove

Atrium White

White Mountain

White Lavender

Diana

Sparkling Peachy Whites

Rose Dust	Mountain Gray	Bridal Gown	Pink Violet

Elizabethan	Percale	Antique White	Orchid Shadow

design consult

THESE ARE THE DREAM COLORS FOR LOVERS OF WHITE. Happy in all lighting situations, good companions to other whites, suitable for trim with any color except for lavender, peachy whites have a soft, heirloom quality about them, and they should not be underestimated. These are the whites of swank New York apartments. They are crispy clean on a wall and perform exceptionally well in artificial light and in windowless spaces. In fact, peachy whites always look pretty.

design consult

WHITES WITH A HINT OF GREEN are perfect with reds, really lovely with soft pinks, and gorgeous with aqua or gray. Whites with green undertones can be very temperamental on the wall, however. They are especially troublesome in sunny rooms or in circumstances where the lighting is mixed. I would avoid them altogether, especially in an entirely white space, except that they are useful for trim in red and green color schemes when a good deal of fabric is present in the room. Never use green-whites in the kitchen, which is generally overly lit and bright, or on a wall in rooms lit by fluorescent bulbs, which will make the color look frosty.

Fresh Green Whites

Nautilus	Alaskan Mist
Winter Walk	Gilded Linen
Kiss Me Kate	Romance
Woodrow Wilson Linen	Pontoon White

Ice Ballet

Morning Cloud

Ash Mist

Tulle White

Evening Light

Extreme White

Cinema Screen

Soft
Gray
Whites

design consult

GRAY-TONED WHITES run the color gamut from parchment to fresh snow. They pair perfectly with peachy whites, are beautiful trim colors, and look splendid on both the walls and ceiling under any lighting conditions—especially in rooms with a northern exposure. If you mix a few gray whites with peachy whites and vary the sheens of the painted surfaces, the entire room will take on an alabaster glow. Gray whites are the ones to use for that quintessential French-inspired all-white room.

Super Whites

Super White

Decorator White

Ultra White

Ceiling Bright White

design consult

CLEARLY SOME "WHITES" CONTAIN A BIT OF COLOR. But those that are tinted this way and that to another subtle version are still considered white. For the closest thing to a pure white, look for one that has been labeled by the manufacturer as "Super" or "Ultra." These whites have a good deal of hide when the paint is a good quality. These pure whites look garish on a wall unless they are surrounded by lots of artwork and enjoy near-perfect lighting conditions. I call them "museum whites," and for the most part, that's where they belong.

Make It Work

Even if you're a dyed-in-the-wool devotee of white walls and ceilings, you may want to take a tiny dip into color by using it as an accent, as you will see in the examples illustrated in this chapter. A little touch here or there isn't terribly risky, but it may be just enough to make your otherwise all-white scheme outstanding. And don't forget, you can add a little

a light lift

in the color hot seat

an artful approach

color with accessories, such as pillows, art, or other objects that you can easily change when you wish. Once you start playing with color accents, you'll be pleasantly surprised to see how using some in a room that's painted white makes the most out of the overall design—and it was so simple to do! Take a look here. The results may surprise you.

on the waterfront

bursts of color

one bedroom, three ways

A Light Lift

Color saves the day

To make all-white less severe without painting, add one warm color accent. In this case, introducing color via the pendant lamps that hang over this table is just enough to warm up the dining room without disturbing the overall, basically neutral scheme.

The three pendants outfitted in topaz-color shades are easy on the eye and collaborate successfully with the incandescent lighting to create a warm glow from above. The color, while fun and invigorating, is one that the eye would expect to encounter from a lighting source. This keeps the glow easy on the eyes.

Atrium White

Topaz

other options

THE SAME PENDANT LIGHTS, this time in an exhilarating synthetic vivid green, will blur the harshness cast by environmentally friendly fluorescent bulbs. The green is a modern interpretation of its organic, mineral green counterpart that acts as an eye-soothing balance to the blue cast of the daylight from the window wall.

Hearty Hosta

COLORLESS GLASS SHADES would not be substantial enough to balance harmoniously with the massive dining table in the room and would appear to float aimlessly in space. However, adding one well-defined color in a repetitive but restrained fashion is a bold stroke of color genius.

Enchanting Ginger

design consult

IF YOU ARE FEELING A LITTLE APPREHENSIVE ABOUT CHOOSING COLOR, take a snapshot of the space and let your computer, colored pencils, or imagination be your decision-making guide. If color solves an existing problem, such as lighting glare from bright-white light, that's all the better. Above all, be deliberate in your choice—and always go for an opaque shade. Clear glass is too harsh on the eyes.

Ultra White	Navajo Red

In the Color Hot Seat

Color saves the day

Aside from changing the cabinets and countertops, there is no simpler way out of an all-white scheme than to add color with furnishings. Here, swapping the white leather seats on the island stools for a natural raw sienna makes this kitchen look earthy and warm.

White is always a popular choice for kitchen cabinets and fixtures because it never gets dated, and it goes with everything. The color on the stools, here, is consistent with finely dyed leathers and harmonizes well with the fruits and vegetables a busy kitchen is apt to have on hand—and often on display. White chairs or counter stools can disappear entirely into white-painted cabinetry and marble countertops, and so calling attention to them by using a pinch of a zesty color may be just what the chef ordered.

BEFORE

another option

LIME GREEN is another choice that is very much at home in any kitchen. This color goes well with the black-and-white floor and backsplash, and beckons to the foliage outdoors. It also has an unexpectedly pleasant conversation with the glass in the cabinet fronts. Glass always has just a hint of green in it somewhere, which is especially noticeable when it is lit, as these cabinets are in the evening. A third option, a bright and strong lemon yellow, would be exhilarating and graphic. But it might look too modern for the traditional lines of this kitchen.

Lime Green

MAKE IT WORK • MAKE IT WOR

An Artful Approach

Color saves the day

Any all-white space can look spare or simply become boring. Either situation is easily solved with art. Warm wood tones live beautifully in all-white situations, yet they benefit greatly from a balancing dash of color.

Neutral accessories that provide a tactile or textural diversion are significant additions to a well-designed white room. Nothing enhances this scheme as effectively as one well-chosen piece of artwork.

COLORFUL COLLECTIONS AND ART add instant panache to different spaces around this home. A collection of handbags (above) brings color into the simple entry hall, and more traditional art—framed prints and paintings (right and opposite top and bottom)—provides added interest in other rooms.

Linen White

Black Truffles

Relic Bronze

Artist Brown

design consult

THINK ABOUT IT: ART GAL-
LERIES AND MUSEUMS rarely
deviate from the convention of
hanging significant art pieces on
all-white walls. That's because
the white background lets the art
take full attention. If you're planning to hang art on your white
wall, take another tip from art
galleries—install proper indirect
lighting. Low-voltage lamps and
fixtures that emit soft, diffused
white light will show off art to its
best advantage, especially if you
can control this light separately
from the room's other sources.

On the Waterfront

Color saves the day

Accents of sophisticated color used with restraint work together with an almost all-white, open-plan kitchen/ dining/family room to create an unobtrusive backdrop for a commanding view of the sea.

The cool, somewhat ambiguous blue-green-gray selected for the chairs here is a refined choice. This is the blue the eye processes almost instinctively as the color of water. It's worth taking extra time in the paint department to find it.

Pale Chambray

Ash Mist

other options

Intense Pink

Blue Note Black

THIS INTENSE PINK is perhaps a little more flowery or candy-colored than mauve. The chairs—and the entire kitchen, for that matter—seem compatible with this dusty, rosy, not-quite-pink. It's a color that is familiar to anyone who enjoys sunsets in South Beach or sunrises in sunny Southern California.

BLACK, on the other hand, suggests a modern, more austere style. The modernity of the kitchen design lends itself to the black, and keeping the higher bar-height stools in their cool and calm gray allows the dining collection some much-deserved attention.

Bursts of Color

Color saves the day

A moderated dose of color is all that was required to bring out the beauty in this kitchen's white cabinetry. Adding varying tones of a single hue, in this case green, does not require any color-matching expertise—a relief to the inhabitants of this divine kitchen.

The accent color has been brought in with the ceramic pieces over the range and as paint on the island, so it will be easy to change. Should the homeowners' penchant for greens begin to wane, they can paint the substantial island in place and swap the pottery for pieces that match their new accent color.

Spring Leaf

Celery Ice

Iced Mint

Antique White

COLORFUL POTTERY, DISHES, COOKWARE, or even countertop appliances are excellent ways for the color-shy to explore their preferences in a somewhat noncommittal way. Many practical kitchen items come in trendy colors today.

another option

I'D LOVE TO SEE THE ISLAND in an earthy brown and the platters in pink, although if you look at the photo on the right, a pretty tomato red is awfully swell, too.

Red Tomato

Rose Wine

Ginger Peachy

Pale Orange

One Bedroom, Three Ways

Color saves the day

Taste and style are easy to depict in a bedroom that's painted crisp and clean. The bedding provides an important and sizable place for style points and a focal point.

Colorful pillows can be re-covered with the seasons or subtracted or fine-tuned to solidify a color story. In this bedroom, the colorful lamp is doing as much for the room as the fabulous comforter. The spare white walls couldn't be more appropriate, or could they?

other options

CONSIDERING THE WOOD TONE OF THE HEADBOARD and the expanse of window and doors, painting the walls an adobe-like red warms up the space and complements the bedding. Note that the singular primary yellow pillow is limiting the potential color options in this room; warm ambers, spicy tangerine, or any color with a peach undertone would clash.

Rose Wine

ADJUSTING THE PILLOW to a warmer yellow opens the door to the gold range of colors that are present in the wood's undertones. A strong, nearly brassy squash color is fabulous with the red bedding and brings the wood to life. This color range, even its most citrus-like versions, is easy on the eyes and comfortable.

Summer Field

THE WARMER YELLOW PILLOW allows you to consider what color this room should be. The western exposure offers a warm afternoon light, and a delicious color made of natural pigments and inspired by the garden looks organic. It resists being identified as simply yellow, orange, or gold, but it might be called golden yellow with a slight orange undertone.

Summer Lily

CHAPTER 7

Effortless

hate to paint?

Color

there are other ways to update or add color

"I hate to paint." How many times have you heard that? Besides, a pink dining room or an orange living room can be a hard sell if there are a number of opinionated voices in your home. Things can get dicey when it's your other half who's on the ladder, moping and complaining that the blue you spent hours choosing looks like the color of a carburetor.

If an enormous swath of color will assault the senses of the more conservative members of the family, there are other means to a color-filled end. Here's how to bring color into a bland room or refresh a dated look— usually without lifting a paintbrush.

CRIMSON ACCENTS that have been judiciously scattered around the room perk up the formerly all-neutral scheme without obliterating its quiet elegance.

Make It Work

This chapter demonstrates how easy it is to bring color into your world. Although painting is an inexpensive way to add the magic, sometimes it isn't necessary. A touch of rich red in accent pieces, for example, provides the perfect level of excitement and design continuity in an off-white room. Subtle garden-inspired colors chosen for chairs freshen the look of a

singular sensation

low key

a jazzy tour-de-force

lavender mist

cream-colored dining room, and hot pink and orange pillows and cushions satisfy one homeowner's desire to throw caution to the wind—but within moderation! And if you don't mind doing just a little bit of painting, see what a difference it makes to apply just a touch of color to "the fifth wall"—the ceiling.

summer party

wake up the bedroom

looking up to color

above reproach

Singular Sensation

Color saves the day

A singular color, used as an accent in this otherwise all-neutral scheme, unites the room's eclectic decorative styles.

Repeating the bold pomegranate red in a rhythmic pattern not only adds color, it also gives the room structure. Movable painted pieces, accessories, unusual artifacts, and picture frames reinforce the color and keep the eye moving from place to place. Using it on various surfaces and textures adds another layer of interest. For example, you'll notice that the quality and personality of the color appears different on the drapery band from how it looks in the red roses.

Frosted Pomegranate

Edwardian Linen

Woodstock Tan

Black Truffles

design consult

TO MAKE AN EXISTING ROOM WITH MANY ELEMENTS FEEL MORE COHESIVE, choose one color and find places to use it throughout the space. It may take some time to get everything settled, but if you have an odd mix of this and that—your French frame, his recliner, and the kids' coloring table—one neat and well-articulated package of a color will pull even the most divisive of design styles together. Accent the monochromatic collection with another single color, and suddenly your big mismatched mess will look planned and eclectic. The more vivid the accent color, the less of it you will need.

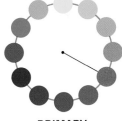

PRIMARY

Low Key

Color saves the day

Black and brown lift up neutral and monochromatic color schemes with understated elegance. Brown is one of those love-it-or-hate-it colors. If you're not fond of brown, you can substitute rich bronze, pale toast, or a buff color, and still create the serene look of this room.

The sophistication of this bedroom is so understated that it's hard to get a fix on what's making the room feel so good and work so well. There is a spare, nearly austere quality to the design that lends a distinctively soothing effect visually. Careful use of the color brown as an accent and a neutral perimeter play a large part in the calmness. The quiet contrast of the chocolate brown and bronze pillows is perfect.

Woodstock Tan

Volcanic Island

Navajo White

other options

OUTFITTING THE BED IN SCARLET RED would be exhilarating, if not as visually quiet as the brown. But don't be surprised or alarmed if the creamy white walls start to look a little green after about 20 seconds of staring at the red bedding. Called an "afterimage," this experience won't last long, fading out after approximately 30 seconds. (See "What the Heck is an 'Afterimage'?" below.)

Candy Cane Red

REPLACING THE BEDDING with a rich and exotic electric blue creates a contrast to the white that is similar to that of the brown. However, again, your eyes will play tricks on you. This time, after a few seconds of looking at the blue, the intensity of that color will fade into its complement—orange—when you gaze at the white wall. Let's face it, the original brown is inviting, and there is no afterimage to upset the calm.

Blueberry Bush

what the heck is an "afterimage"?

AN AFTERIMAGE IS AN OPTICAL ILLUSION. It occurs when your eyes' photoreceptors become overstimulated by a color so that when you look away from it, you see its complement, or opposite. The effect is most perceivable if you look at the color for up to a minute and then fix your gaze on a white surface. But, generally, an afterimage is almost imperceptible because it's brief. Quickly, your color memory kicks in, and you perceive the color in its original, actual form.

These intriguing apparitions happen rather easily and all the time, but our brains just filter out the information in our day-to-day lives. However, we do sense this slightly in our color perceptions, particu-

larly in a white room. You might let this guide you when you choose paint colors, especially for rooms that are open to one another. Try using a progression of complementary colors, and you'll see how comfortable they feel. ("Oh, I'm moving through yellow; now here I am in violet; and then, what a lovely green!") Afterimage also helps to explain why discordant color arrangements are disturbing—they feel unnatural.

To understand the afterimage experience, try this: stare at the yellow box, left, for about 20 seconds, and then look at a blank sheet of white paper. You will see a phantom image of the box, only now it will appear to be yellow's complement, which is violet.

Summer Party

Color saves the day

Just a hint of color on the chairs adds fresh vitality to this dining room. The room's soft yellow hues are tantalizing paired with the purity of a clear aqua.

The clarity of this particular shade of crisp aqua, which is not blue or green, boggles the mind. It falls on the edge of blue or green, making it a cusp color. As such, it can hold your attention while you consider the depth, origin, and richness of the hue, which is so lucid you can't look away. Limiting the aqua to only two chairs here is compelling—your eyes will crave more of it. That's a promise.

Aqua	Minced Onion	Rainforest Dew	Pale Avocado

design consult

THERE IS BROWN IN THIS ROOM, minding its business as usual in the well-waxed and glowing wood tones of the table and floor. I think the most important element the designer took care to address concerns the chair legs; keeping them an unobtrusive sandy white creates a long and uninterrupted line of color straight up and down the chairs' edge while the garden-inspired colors sit just like flowers above the foliage.

THE SOFT KID-SKIN CHAIRS shimmer like sunlit sand in the light of the day. The complexity of the understated yellow-white tinged with just a hint of green reduces the contrast between the chairs and keeps the long expanse of shapes, forms, and colors from appearing unsettling.

THE CHAIRS' FRINGE incorporates some of the other colors in the room. It's a small but significant detail.

TERTIARY

Flaxseed

Fresh Cut Grass

Pear Green

Stem Green

Bay Sands

Wake up the Bedroom

Color saves the day

A soft yellow hue on the walls in this room, opposite, is pleasant in the morning sunlight. But the purity of the linens and the simplicity of the bed left the room a little too reserved. The addition of yellow-green draperies provides a filter for the early light and makes the yellow appear a bit brighter. Now the room has a discernable palette that was not created entirely by the fabric but is strongly supported by it.

Playing up the yellow-green background of the curtains with a nearly discordant green-on-green plaid, two simple pillows tie together what is a newly yellow-and-green combination. The beige upholstered headboard and creamy white bedding no longer need to carry the overall design, and so they settle back nicely into the supporting role for which they are better suited.

FABRICS CONTAINING DIFFERENT TONES OF PINK add a finishing touch to this bedroom. They also heighten the pink tones in the pale wall color and draw out the red in the wood's finish.

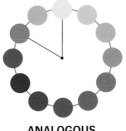

ANALOGOUS

design consult

TELL YOUR COLOR STORY WITH FABRIC. I've had more than a few discussions with clients who bemoan the cost of luxurious fabrics—or any kind of fabrics for that matter, be they silk or hemp. If there's a debate in your household, ask the naysayer to consider this: does it cost more to paint a room pink or to add pink pillows? And point out that a window treatment is really a necessity in the bedroom. Once you win over your opposition, you can create an intoxicating color combination in a richly textured, acoustically pleasing, and sumptuous room of color that nobody had to paint. (You're welcome!)

A Jazzy Tour de Force

Color saves the day

This room is a divine example of how accenting with a snappy combination of accent colors—ones that would look loud on a wall—come together with delightfully appealing ease in an entirely neutral room. Remove all the colorful pillows and cushions and you have a room that is still undeniably beautiful, but without the verve and vitality these colors create.

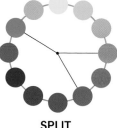

SPLIT
COMPLEMENTARY

Green is playing a supporting role to the hot, saturated fuchsia and mango combination, but it is a necessary one. Offering a complementary reference to the heat, or chroma, of the fuchsia, the understated green accents appear effortless. Flowers and small-scale accessories, for that matter anything portable, can be used to advance a color without shouting "look at me." Repeating the cream pillows and tying them to the fuchsia and mango with trim helps keep the look from boiling over the top.

design consult

THE BLACK IS A BIG DEAL IN THIS ROOM. Without it, the horizontal plane of vivid fuchsia at the window seat would feel as if it were coming after you. Hot, saturated, high-intensity colors advance like nobody's business, and they need a strong element to keep them grounded. Brown would have worked, but the black is better; the high contrast says "wow" and provides an opportunity for the next element of design genius, the little seat. Upholstered in a print that captures the eye, it is the most outstanding pattern in this corner of the room. While the hot colors all advance with an incredible amount of rhythm, the distraction of the busy little print provides some visual balance.

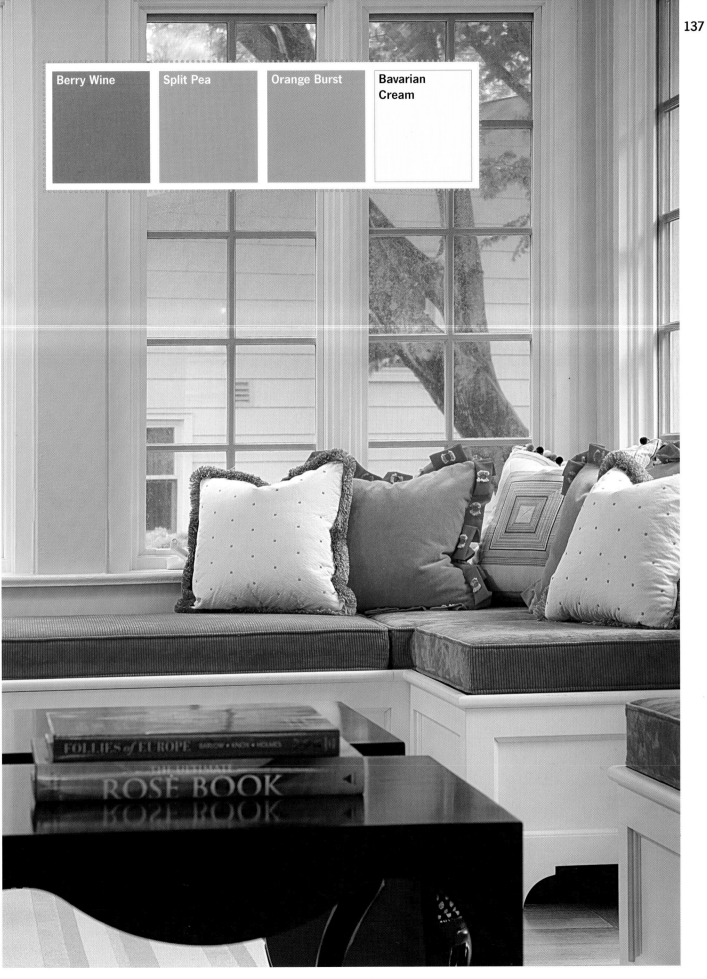

Berry Wine

Split Pea

Orange Burst

Bavarian Cream

LUXURY HOUSES CITY

Lavender Mist

Color saves the day

Soft color introduced with fabric is a perfect way to counterbalance a room with strong architectural features. The space is large, but the soft color palette of warm gray-lavenders, lichen greens, and sweet lilacs is inviting. Mixing stripes, solids, florals, and abstract prints works beautifully because the colors coordinate so well.

Feminine and French, this inspired sitting room is pretty, but not overly so. This is partly due to the strong linear and symmetrical features of the space, but it's also because the designer paid careful attention to scale. The daybed has been recessed into a draped alcove, which helps to make the grand space feel intimate. Oversize chairs add presence and balance the mass of the warm lilac draperies, which will cool down to a beautiful shade of lavender blue liatris as the daylight disappears.

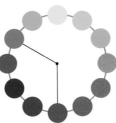

SECONDARY

Lavender Lipstick	**Beach Plum**	**Raspberry Ice**
Dark Linen	**Pale Sea Mist**	**Dill Pickle**

WITH LOTS OF PAINTED PANELING, this room needs the touch of delicate colors and soft fabrics to make it feminine.

design consult

PURPLE AND GREEN are two colors that are easy on the eye. Rooms seem to float in their presence, especially when the purple is softened to a pale, atmospheric lilac or lavender. I could write an entire book on the subject of lavender. It is a complex color that I would like to see used more often. There are very few other colors that wouldn't benefit from a little lavender accent. Delicate gray-lavenders have a tendency to shift under varying lighting conditions. This gives them an ethereal quality. Modern synthetic pigments shift less. While this makes their color formulations more definitive, sadly the rooms where they appear lack mood. You can't "fix" lavender, however. It needs too many tints. This makes lavender an elusive, independent wanderer that can ramble in, around, and through complex color palettes as quietly as the mist it emulates.

Looking Up to Color

Color saves the day

There is some merit to putting color on a ceiling—even if that means painting. OK, no color will reflect sunlight better than white. But faced with heavy furniture they didn't want to move and a wallcovering they preferred to retain, the owners of this home decided to add color to the ceiling. Crazy? No. The color gave the room a needed boost and looks terrific.

This tongue-and-groove ceiling is interesting in itself in this charming countrified bedroom. Keeping to a color that harmonizes with the walls, the owners chose a soft butter cream. This delicate color is almost white, but not quite. It picks up one of the colors in the wallpaper, which is why it is so successful. If you do this, you may be tempted to add color to every ceiling in your house. My advice? Don't do it. Once really is enough.

Butter Cream

Olive

Coral Pink

Black Truffles

another option

The owners could have tried a fresh mint green for the ceiling. It's a brighter, cleaner version of the green in the wallcovering and adds a lovely contrast to the colorful warmth of the handmade heirloom quilts that drape the bed.

Surfside

design consult

THE ABILITY OF A CEILING TO REFLECT SUNLIGHT is either enhanced or diminished by the Light Reflective Value (LRV) of the paint. The LRV is a rating assigned to paint that indicates the percentage of light the color will reflect. Your paint dealer can help you choose a color with an LRV that is suitable for the ceiling. Also, some manufacturers note the LRV value on the color card. Unusually bright whites have a LRV of 90 percent, and toned whites, which appear to be crisp and clean and quite white, are generally assigned a rating of around 75 percent. The color selected for this room and the one chosen for the room on the next page are pale tints that fall between the 50–70 percent LRV. That's enough to keep a ceiling looking bright and colorful at the same time.

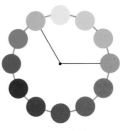

TERTIARY

Bennington Gray

Farmhouse Red

Derby Brown

Split Pea

Above Reproach

Color saves the day

When it's in a period house, updating a room's color palette can be a little tricky. In this case, the only change needed was a color accent—on the ceiling. It gently updates the look while maintaining the room's vintage charm. The green on the shades and the choice of color scheme, while less true to the period, harmonize with the vocabulary of the room. This is a study in simple design that is easier to love than achieve.

I like the authenticity of this room, which was built a century ago. The high windows, the wallpaper, and the furnishings speak to a timeless heritage in a very honest and unusually easy manner. Adding a drab putty or soft smoky gray on the ceiling reflects the essence of the antique cherry floor and respects both the design and the era of the home. (See "Another Option," below right.)

design consult

THE ART OF UNDERSTATEMENT is not always mastered easily. However, this room is an excellent example of it. A spirited vintage wallcovering paired with a neutral gray adds energy and scale to the room without overwhelming the eye. If the ceiling was repainted an earthy yellow or duck's egg blue, it would be too much; the room is sunny as is, and the gray will make it appear even more so—but just enough.

another option

Bennington Gray

THE EXTRA HINT of color provided by painting the ceiling uplifts the mood of the room.

COMPLEMENTARY

what's in

here's what the color experts

the Forecast?

see for the new decade

Every year, professional color forecasters release their palettes, assessments, and predictions for the year of color ahead and beyond. I think color forecasters have a really fabulous job. Employed by huge paint companies, textile manufacturers, marketing companies, enormous media conglomerates, and the entire graphic arts community, color forecasters are a group to take seriously. They follow clues from the fashion industry, cultural trends, consumer buying habits, and professionals in the home-design community. The colors in this chapter are some of the ones you'll be seeing a lot of next year—and for the next decade.

TRADITION WITH A TWIST is a recurring theme in contemporary decorating. The pink-and-green color scheme puts a modern spin on the room's traditional architecture and furnishings.

Make It Work

Many of the color forecasts for the new decade are for intense, saturated hues, as well as for neutrals, with green considered a part of the latter category. While every color has its merit and place, very warm or hot colors will make a room appear smaller than it is. Pairing stark white with blue is timeless, and you can dress up the look with yellow, brown,

color and shimmer

go for the gold

perfection in gold, blue, and brown

orange, red, purple, and even green as trends evolve and color revolutions are fought. Because a color scheme is as much about the feeling it conveys as it is about looks, don't weigh yourself down in too many specific trends. If "your blue" isn't one of the trendy shades, go with what you like. Not crazy about brown? Use camel. Keep it personal.

amazing in amethyst

pink prediction

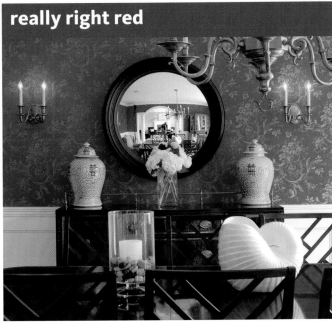
really right red

Color and Shimmer

Color saves the day

An au courant collection of sophisticated, clear, and saturated colors has an international flair and architectural sharpness about it. When combined in a room, as in this skillfully designed dining room, the seeting feels chic, European, and classic.

Certainly there is a mastery here that supercedes a collection of several colors, but the understated effects, from the windows dressed in celestial blue draperies to the subtle repetition of an enticing rose hue and shimmery materials, turn a seemingly difficult palette into an effortless and serene collaboration.

Celestial Blue

Musket Brown

White Vanilla

Blushing Red

New Black

design consult

BLACK AND A COOL GREEN-ISH PEAT-MOSS BROWN fulfill the need of neutrals in this room, and the gold is represented in honest gilt, warm lighting, and natural sisal. The formality of the room is made so much more inviting because of the restraint of the draperies; if there were more of them (covering the French doors, for example), the room would seem to be blue.

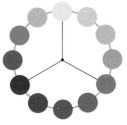

PRIMARY

MAKE IT WORK • MAKE IT WORK • MAKE IT WORK • MAKE IT WORK

Go for the Gold

Color saves the day

When the owners of this house were looking for a new wall color for their family room, they decided that a strong, warm gold was the way to go. An imposing stone fireplace runs from the floor to the room's double-high ceiling. Gold is a color that is present in stone—both real and man-made—especially if the stone has been subjected to water for a while. The gold here is a natural color derived from an ochre pigment. Because this oxide-influenced hue occurs in forests, streams, rivers, and fields, it feels familiar and natural. That's why gold pairs so well with stone, whether it's wet, dry, natural, or even a synthetic or composite rendition.

Mustard gold has an organic quality about it. The color feels sunlit, but it lacks the sweetness or charm of yellow, something the homeowners didn't want. Pumpkin orange is terrific with a gold palette, so they used it on an accent chair. If they want to make a switch next year, they might accent the room a sapphire blue or jewel-tone turquoise. Either color would look smashing paired with this gold.

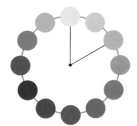

Mustard Gold

Pumpkin Orange

Black Brown

Warm White

ANALOGOUS

BROWN, SQUASH, AND GRASSY ORGANIC GREENS that have no blue undertones all get along beautifully with our new best friend—complicated gold. If you are using a lot of brown in the mix, make it a chocolate reddish brown, and don't be afraid to use a lot of it—the gold can hold its own in the company of rich dark browns, tangy oranges, and any red.

design consult

WHETHER MUTED, BRASSY, SHARP, or the color of mustard, gold has a universal, multicultural, and even international appeal. From the point of view of a colorist, gold is the product of elaborate, well-considered tinting formulas, with red, green, brown, black, and sometimes even a little blue added to the mix. Decidedly complex, gold is deeply saturated and looks rich. However, gold will change drastically in varying lighting conditions. Luckily, it looks good in a room that has been lit with the new energy-efficient compact fluorescent bulbs everyone is using now. Gold's red tones are the perfect foil to the green-tinged light that these bulbs tend to cast.

Perfection in Pale Gold, Blue, and Brown

Color saves the day

In a master bedroom, a designer used a "cool" version of gold to create a look that is rich but not harsh. This version of gold is soft, pale, and less saturated than the mustard on the wall on page 150.

A calm shade of blue that was chosen for the coverlet balances perfectly with the gold. Touches of brown in the pillows, the upholstered ottoman, and the wood tones of the furniture keep the room from looking too feminine. For contrast, the designer upholstered the headboard in a clean, soft white that stands out against the gold wall. Shimmery silver accents call out every hint of blue.

THE CONTRAST between the warmth of brown and the coolness of blue is attractive. It's used in just the right amount to support, rather than detract from, the gold scheme.

Pale Gold	Weathered Linen	Chocolate Brown

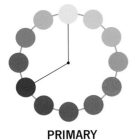

PRIMARY

design consult

WOULD YOU PAINT A ROOM THAT IS INTENDED FOR REST GOLD? As you can see in this bedroom, gold walls will not disturb the peace if you choose a version of the color that is soft and has a bit of green in it. That's why the color scheme works so well here. Of course, the amount of natural light that a room receives can intensify golden tones, so try out a sample or two of your choice before you paint. If you need to keep out the light during the early morning or afternoon, install a sun-block-lined fabric treatment, blinds, or shutters.

Amazing Amethyst

Plum Good

Mauvelous

Pale Lilac Gray

Amazing in Amethyst

Color saves the day

Looking for something high-fashion and less predictable, this homeowner selected an amethyst palette for her bedroom. A long-neglected color, purple is making a comeback—all of its variations, including lilac, lavender, even mauve, are right smack dab in the forefront of colors that professional authorities consider to be of the moment.

Any purple is a nice accent to any of the golds, but as you can see, it can stand alone with dignity.

I've noticed a lot of men in purple ties lately, so it won't be much longer before you see it everywhere.

design consult

PURPLE WAS ONCE THE RAREST AND MOST PRIZED of colors, reserved for royalty. Its popularity has come and gone and come again over the decades. Now again, purple is having a renaissance. Although the color has traditionally been reserved for private spaces in the home, particularly bedrooms, its highly individual quality is making it an attractive choice for other areas inside and outside the home today. Baby boomers take note: purple's red component makes it flattering to skin tones.

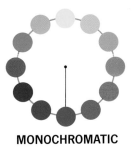

MONOCHROMATIC

AN EXCELLENT EYE and a careful hand were needed to put together this amazing color scheme of vivacious violet, earthy brown, and a yellow-green.

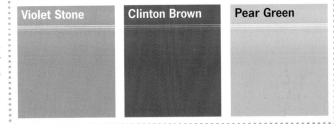

| Violet Stone | Clinton Brown | Pear Green |

Really Right Red

Color saves the day

The owners knew they wanted a red dining room, opposite, but they weren't sure about how to pick "the right red." Instead of painting the walls, they decided to install a tone-on-tone floral pattern in the clearest, brightest red of all: scarlet.

Red has a long-standing place of honor in the dining room. Early in my decorative painting career I glazed so many red dining rooms that I mixed the glazes in 5-gallon quantities and still never had enough of it. You won't grow tired of red; everyone looks lovely surrounded by it, and it is a convivial color.

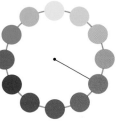

PRIMARY

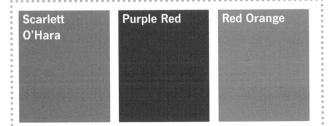

Scarlett O'Hara	Purple Red	Red Orange

design consult

THERE IS A QUEST IN THE DESIGN COMMUNITY for the perfect red. It's a never-ending, never-satisfied kind of thing that is, in my experience, specific to red. Garnet, crimson, cherry, ravishing, lipstick, scarlet, cinnabar—the list goes on and on. If you love red, close your eyes and pick one—you will not be disappointed. As for the forecast reds, right now shades that are derived from the sharper magenta or carmine range of tints are in demand, but don't tell that to these scarlet lovers.

IF YOU'RE A LITTLE TENTATIVE about your red pursuits, a chair rail will provide you with a safety zone until your sensibilities catch up to this color. All reds look smashing with white, and especially so when the white is as pure as a cotton ball and the red is a very deep purple-red.

A COOL GRAY-GREEN, such as the one used on the window trim, pairs beautifully with the medium red-orange persimmon of the bedding. It's an unexpected combination that works well here.

Pink Prediction

$Color$ saves the day

Looking for something fresh, this designer pulled together a new palette—one that is very much in vogue—for this living room. The dominant color is a pink coral. This color is not an easy sell if there's a man around the house, but if you have a willing companion, it can be stunning with the right accents.

Clearly, this designer possesses a talent that exceeds an ability to present us with a few pretty colored squares. I could write another book to highlight the lessons to be learned in this room. I am delighted to include it here, not only because it is in keeping with the color forecast for the new decade but because it will encourage more than a few admirers to try this upbeat combination in their own homes.

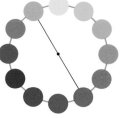

design consult

THE ESSENCE OF THIS ROOM IS PRETTY. To add a little balance, there are a number of handsome accents—most notably black—that keep the room comfortable and approachable. The tactile fabrics add weight to the color scheme, and the line of the sofa is not fussy or frilly. Yet a reserved quality comes from something that has nothing at all to do with the fashionable color scheme—it's the symmetry. The orderly placement of pairs, the accessories, the pillows, and the architecture all work to make this the kind of room everyone can enjoy.

COMPLEMENTARY

Pink Coral

Celery Stick

Black Suede

swatch-o-rama

The following "swatches" represent some of the latest colors offered by several leading manufacturers. For accuracy, however, you should check actual paint chips and consult your paint dealer or the paint experts in your local home-improvement center. Also, test a color under the lighting conditions in the room in which you plan to use it.

BLUES

BEHR
Navy Blue

BENJAMIN MOORE
Faded Denim

GLIDDEN
Phantom Blue

RALPH LAUREN
Dennison Blue

SHERWIN-WILLIAMS
Countrified Blue

VALSPAR
Lapis

BEHR
Windjammer

SHERWIN-WILLIAMS
Veronica Blue

GLIDDEN
Azure Afternoon

VALSPAR
Indigo Lake

RALPH LAUREN
Bimini

BENJAMIN MOORE
California Breeze

BEHR
Liquid Blue

BENJAMIN MOORE
Paddington Blue

GLIDDEN
Jazz Blue

RALPH LAUREN
Regatta

BLUES

VALSPAR
Bonnie Blue

SHERWIN-WILLIAMS
Quiet Refuge

GLIDDEN
Wildflower Wind

BENJAMIN MOORE
Twilight Blue

BEHR
Jamaican Blue

RALPH LAUREN
Breaker

VALSPAR
Rainy Day

BENJAMIN MOORE
Bayberry Blue

BEHR
Tahoe

GLIDDEN
Surf

SHERWIN-WILLIAMS
Basin Street Blue

VALSPAR
Blue Jewel

BENJAMIN MOORE
Light Blue

RALPH LAUREN
Oyster Bay

BEHR
Artesian Water

GLIDDEN
Harbor Light

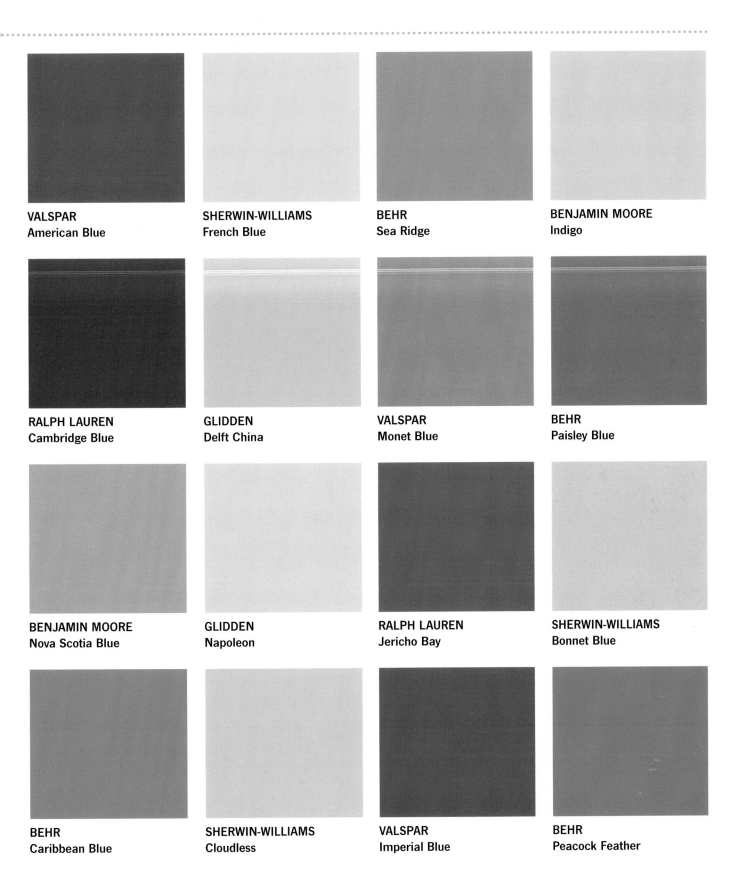

VALSPAR
American Blue

SHERWIN-WILLIAMS
French Blue

BEHR
Sea Ridge

BENJAMIN MOORE
Indigo

RALPH LAUREN
Cambridge Blue

GLIDDEN
Delft China

VALSPAR
Monet Blue

BEHR
Paisley Blue

BENJAMIN MOORE
Nova Scotia Blue

GLIDDEN
Napoleon

RALPH LAUREN
Jericho Bay

SHERWIN-WILLIAMS
Bonnet Blue

BEHR
Caribbean Blue

SHERWIN-WILLIAMS
Cloudless

VALSPAR
Imperial Blue

BEHR
Peacock Feather

BLUES

BEHR
Enchanting

BENJAMIN MOORE
Athens Blue

GLIDDEN
Gulfside

RALPH LAUREN
Lap Pool Blue

SHERWIN-WILLIAMS
Jacaranda

VALSPAR
Ocean Deep

GLIDDEN
Bluebell

RALPH LAUREN
Rugby Blue

BENJAMIN MOORE
Rocky Mountain Sky

SHERWIN-WILLIAMS
Medley Blue

BEHR
Turquoise Blue

VALSPAR
Blueberry Pie

GLIDDEN
Baltic Blue

RALPH LAUREN
Beach Road

BENJAMIN MOORE
Summer Blue

BEHR
Cobalt Flame

REDS

VALSPAR
Oh So Red

SHERWIN-WILLIAMS
Feverish Pink

RALPH LAUREN
Duke Red

GLIDDEN
Strawberry Crush

BENJAMIN MOORE
Ladybug Red

BEHR
Chili Pepper

SHERWIN-WILLIAMS
Valentine

VALSPAR
Classic Red

RALPH LAUREN
Mission Wildflower

GLIDDEN
Riding Hood

BENJAMIN MOORE
Smoldering Red

BEHR
Poinsettia

SHERWIN-WILLIAMS
Fifties Pink

VALSPAR
Brick Facade

RALPH LAUREN
Castillian Pink

GLIDDEN
Cranberry Zing

REDS ....

BENJAMIN MOORE
Warm Comfort

BEHR
Firecracker

SHERWIN-WILLIAMS
Lusty Red

VALSPAR
Terra Cotta Red

GLIDDEN
Rose Kiss

RALPH LAUREN
University Red

BENJAMIN MOORE
Coral Bronze

BEHR
Sachet

VALSPAR
Hacienda Tile

SHERWIN-WILLIAMS
Dragon Fruit

GLIDDEN
Flaming Sword

RALPH LAUREN
Aspen Orange

BEHR
Red Tomato

VALSPAR
Savannah Red

BENJAMIN MOORE
Shy Cherry

SHERWIN-WILLIAMS
Daredevil

GLIDDEN
Pink Tiger

BENJAMIN MOORE
Million Dollar Red

VALSPAR
Cupid

SHERWIN-WILLIAMS
Kirsch Red

RALPH LAUREN
Tucson

GLIDDEN
Deep Pleasure

BEHR
Deep Bloom

BENJAMIN MOORE
Claret Rose

SHERWIN-WILLIAMS
Daring

VALSPAR
Heirloom Red

RALPH LAUREN
Anthem Red

GLIDDEN
Tender Rose

BEHR
Cardinal

BENJAMIN MOORE
Gypsy Rose

SHERWIN-WILLIAMS
Fireworks

VALSPAR
Red Ochre

VIOLETS

BEHR
Royal Intrigue

BENJAMIN MOORE
Mighty Aphrodite

GLIDDEN
Versailles

RALPH LAUREN
Colombine

SHERWIN-WILLIAMS
Plumb

VALSPAR
Grape Slush

BENJAMIN MOORE
Amethyst Shadow

GLIDDEN
Astor

RALPH LAUREN
Quarry

BEHR
Viking Purple

SHERWIN-WILLIAMS
African Violet

VALSPAR
Water Iris

GLIDDEN
Purple Sage

BENJAMIN MOORE
Freesia

RALPH LAUREN
Deep Indigo

BEHR
Elite

VALSPAR
Easter Parade

BEHR
Rich Purple

GLIDDEN
Frill

BENJAMIN MOORE
Purple Rain

RALPH LAUREN
Chinese Hibiscus

SHERWIN-WILLIAMS
Borage

VALSPAR
Purplicious

GLIDDEN
Deep Lilac

BENJAMIN MOORE
Seduction

BEHR
Vintage Nickel

RALPH LAUREN
Violet Jewels

VALSPAR
Mountain Majesty

SHERWIN-WILLIAMS
Corsican Purple

GLIDDEN
Purple Passion

BENJAMIN MOORE
French Lilac

BEHR
Meadow Violet

ORANGES

BEHR
Orange Burst

BENJAMIN MOORE
Sweet Orange

GLIDDEN
Sizzle

RALPH LAUREN
Peachtree

SHERWIN-WILLIAMS
Kumquat

VALSPAR
Jack-O'-Lantern

BEHR
Chai Spice

GLIDDEN
Iroquois

RALPH LAUREN
California Poppy

BENJAMIN MOORE
Orange Juice

VALSPAR
Golden Nectar

SHERWIN-WILLIAMS
Valencia

BEHR
Whispering Peach

GLIDDEN
Marigold Blossom

SHERWIN-WILLIAMS
Robust Orange

BENJAMIN MOORE
Peach Sorbet

RALPH LAUREN
Pennant Orange

VALSPAR
Bumblebee

BEHR
Bright Citrus

BENJAMIN MOORE
Goldfish

GLIDDEN
Golden Gate

RALPH LAUREN
Hunter Orange

SHERWIN-WILLIAMS
Sunset

VALSPAR
Halloween

BENJAMIN MOORE
Citrus Blast

BEHR
Orange Grove

GLIDDEN
Whispy Peach

RALPH LAUREN
Outrigger Orange

VALSPAR
Caramel Cream

SHERWIN-WILLIAMS
Autumnal

BEHR
Macaw

BENJAMIN MOORE
Sweet Cardamom

ORANGES

GLIDDEN
Dragonfly

BEHR
Aurora Orange

SHERWIN-WILLIAMS
Minaret Melon

VALSPAR
Mark Twain Peach

BENJAMIN MOORE
Piñata

BEHR
Fiesta Orange

GLIDDEN
Orange Ice

SHERWIN-WILLIAMS
Emberglow

VALSPAR
Arizona Sunset

SHERWIN-WILLIAMS
Outgoing Orange

BENJAMIN MOORE
Mandarin Orange

SHERWIN-WILLIAMS
Gladiola

BEHR
Cantaloupe Slice

GLIDDEN
Crenshaw

BEHR
Electric Orange

VALSPAR
Orange Toffee

YELLOWS ....

BEHR
Bicycle Yellow

BENJAMIN MOORE
Golden Groves

GLIDDEN
Zest

RALPH LAUREN
Goldfinch

SHERWIN-WILLIAMS
Funky Yellow

VALSPAR
Dandelion

BEHR
Lively Yellow

GLIDDEN
That 70s Color

RALPH LAUREN
Gerbera Daisy

VALSPAR
Canary Yellow

BENJAMIN MOORE
Popcorn Kernel

SHERWIN-WILLIAMS
Radiance

GLIDDEN
Sun Rays

BENJAMIN MOORE
Banana Yellow

BEHR
Texas Rose

VALSPAR
Candle Glow

YELLOWS

SHERWIN-WILLIAMS
Forsythia

RALPH LAUREN
Chesapeake Sunset

BEHR
Equator Glow

BENJAMIN MOORE
Limelight

GLIDDEN
Sundrenched

RALPH LAUREN
Pale Straw Yellow

SHERWIN-WILLIAMS
Lemon Twist

VALSPAR
Daisy Shimmer

BENJAMIN MOORE
Lemon Grass

BEHR
Yellow Brick Road

GLIDDEN
Rustic Drama

RALPH LAUREN
Maize

VALSPAR
Pineapple Delight

SHERWIN-WILLIAMS
Lemonade

BEHR
Sunflower

BENJAMIN MOORE
Sunny Days

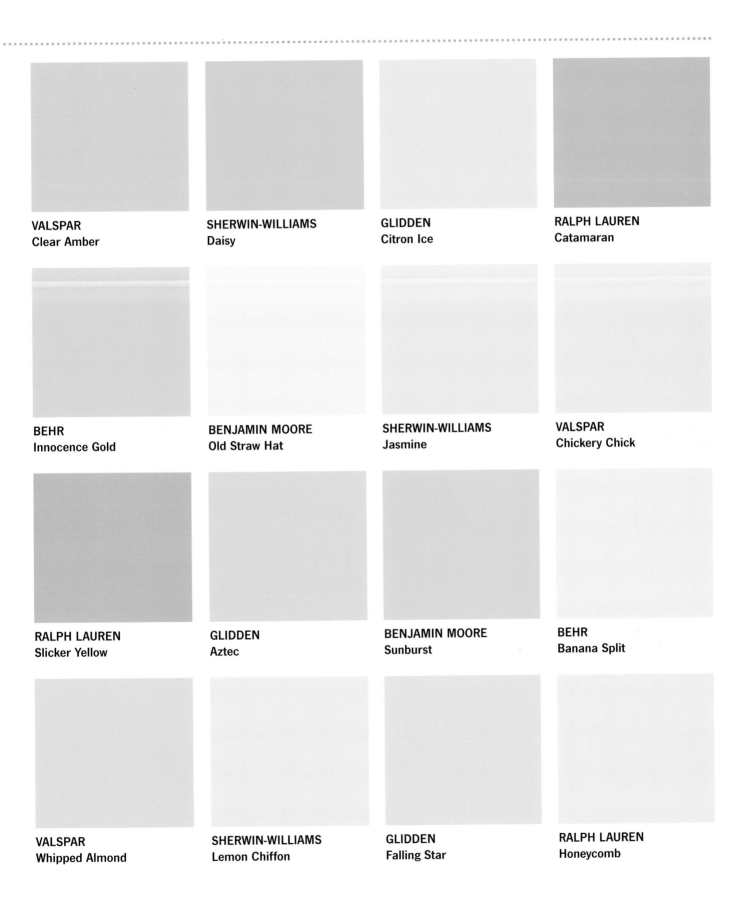

VALSPAR
Clear Amber

SHERWIN-WILLIAMS
Daisy

GLIDDEN
Citron Ice

RALPH LAUREN
Catamaran

BEHR
Innocence Gold

BENJAMIN MOORE
Old Straw Hat

SHERWIN-WILLIAMS
Jasmine

VALSPAR
Chickery Chick

RALPH LAUREN
Slicker Yellow

GLIDDEN
Aztec

BENJAMIN MOORE
Sunburst

BEHR
Banana Split

VALSPAR
Whipped Almond

SHERWIN-WILLIAMS
Lemon Chiffon

GLIDDEN
Falling Star

RALPH LAUREN
Honeycomb

GREENS

VALSPAR
Pea Pod

SHERWIN-WILLIAMS
Lagoon

RALPH LAUREN
Golf Green

GLIDDEN
Tropical Tides

BENJAMIN MOORE
Malachy Green

BEHR
Intense Jade

GLIDDEN
Tempting Teal

VALSPAR
Meadow Mist

RALPH LAUREN
Track Green

SHERWIN-WILLIAMS
Spearmint

BEHR
Fresh Pine

BENJAMIN MOORE
Forest Hills Green

GLIDDEN
Noel

RALPH LAUREN
Oura Green

SHERWIN-WILLIAMS
Green Crystal

VALSPAR
Laguna Green

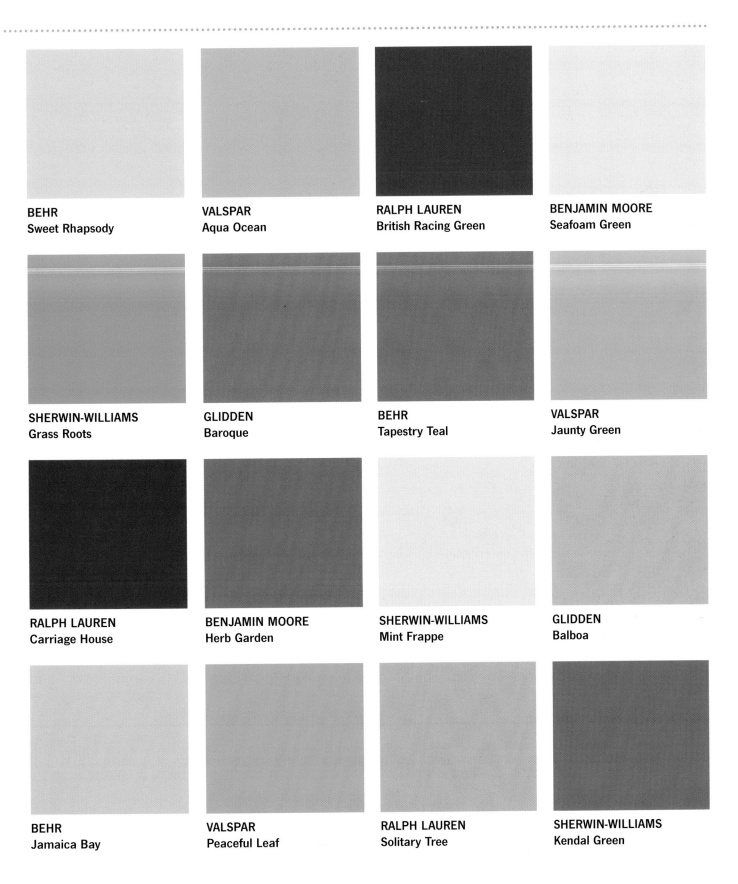

BEHR
Sweet Rhapsody

VALSPAR
Aqua Ocean

RALPH LAUREN
British Racing Green

BENJAMIN MOORE
Seafoam Green

SHERWIN-WILLIAMS
Grass Roots

GLIDDEN
Baroque

BEHR
Tapestry Teal

VALSPAR
Jaunty Green

RALPH LAUREN
Carriage House

BENJAMIN MOORE
Herb Garden

SHERWIN-WILLIAMS
Mint Frappe

GLIDDEN
Balboa

BEHR
Jamaica Bay

VALSPAR
Peaceful Leaf

RALPH LAUREN
Solitary Tree

SHERWIN-WILLIAMS
Kendal Green

GREENS

VALSPAR
Greenery

BENJAMIN MOORE
Paradise Hills Green

BEHR
Sweet Midori

RALPH LAUREN
Teal Forest

SHERWIN-WILLIAMS
Wild Lime

GLIDDEN
Tern

BENJAMIN MOORE
Mill Springs Blue

BEHR
Jungle Trail

VALSPAR
Aqua Glow

SHERWIN-WILLIAMS
Parrot

RALPH LAUREN
Mojave Horizon

GLIDDEN
Dolphin

BENJAMIN MOORE
Peacock Blue

BEHR
Bamboo Leaf

VALSPAR
Icy Mint

SHERWIN-WILLIAMS
Calico

BROWNS & NEUTRALS

VALSPAR
Brown Derby

SHERWIN-WILLIAMS
Kilim Beige

RALPH LAUREN
Stonewall

GLIDDEN
New Suede

BENJAMIN MOORE
Maryville Brown

BEHR
Cup of Cocoa

GLIDDEN
Tootsie

SHERWIN-WILLIAMS
Horse Chestnut

RALPH LAUREN
Pavillion

VALSPAR
Cliff

BENJAMIN MOORE
Smoked Oyster

BEHR
Mauve Nougat

GLIDDEN
Bronze Amulet

RALPH LAUREN
Bridle

SHERWIN-WILLIAMS
Bagel

VALSPAR
Pale Umber

BROWNS & NEUTRALS

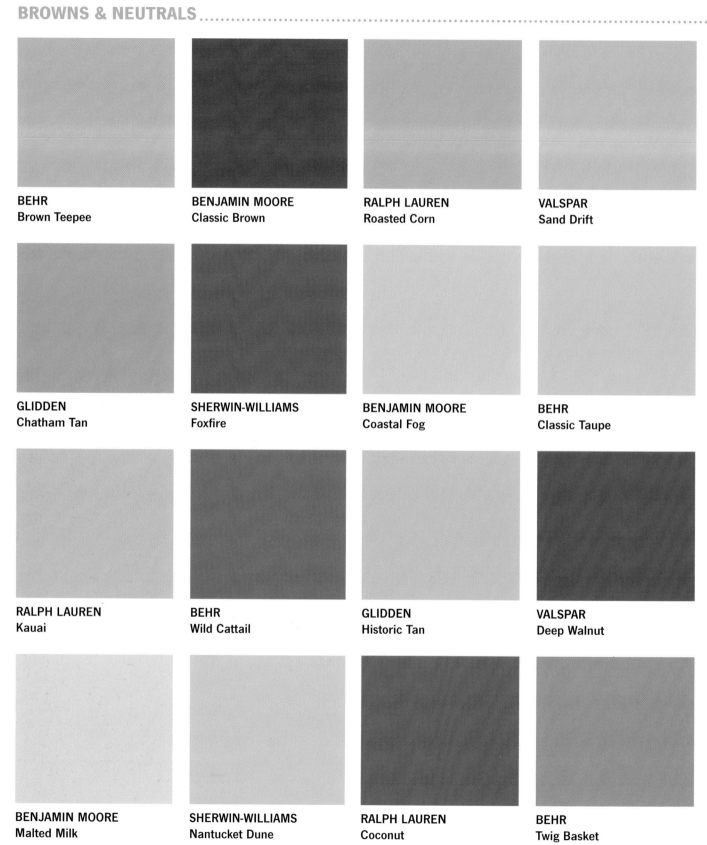

BEHR
Brown Teepee

BENJAMIN MOORE
Classic Brown

RALPH LAUREN
Roasted Corn

VALSPAR
Sand Drift

GLIDDEN
Chatham Tan

SHERWIN-WILLIAMS
Foxfire

BENJAMIN MOORE
Coastal Fog

BEHR
Classic Taupe

RALPH LAUREN
Kauai

BEHR
Wild Cattail

GLIDDEN
Historic Tan

VALSPAR
Deep Walnut

BENJAMIN MOORE
Malted Milk

SHERWIN-WILLIAMS
Nantucket Dune

RALPH LAUREN
Coconut

BEHR
Twig Basket

BENJAMIN MOORE
Stardust

GLIDDEN
Bark

VALSPAR
Warm Buff

SHERWIN-WILLIAMS
Interactive Cream

BEHR
Parfait Cocoa

RALPH LAUREN
Cottonwood

GLIDDEN
Longhorn Brown

BENJAMIN MOORE
Pebble Stone

SHERWIN-WILLIAMS
Otter

VALSPAR
Harvest Brown

BEHR
Tuscan Beige

RALPH LAUREN
Bloody Lily

GLIDDEN
Briarwood

BENJAMIN MOORE
Lenox Tan

VALSPAR
Clay Dusk

BEHR
Fossil Stone

BLACKS & GRAYS ....

BEHR
Black Sable

BENJAMIN MOORE
Aegean Teal

GLIDDEN
Ascot

RALPH LAUREN
Amazon

SHERWIN WILLIAMS
Andiron

VALSPAR
Asphalt

BEHR
Coal

BENJAMIN MOORE
Black Horizon

GLIDDEN
Cormorant

RALPH LAUREN
Black Truffles

SHERWIN-WILLIAMS
Black Fox

VALSPAR
Black Forest

BEHR
Dark as Night

BENJAMIN MOORE
Black Knight

GLIDDEN
Dark Cavern

RALPH LAUREN
Marble

SHERWIN-WILLIAMS
Black Magic

VALSPAR
Canopy

BENJAMIN MOORE
Soft Chinchilla

SHERWIN-WILLIAMS
Cityscape

BEHR
Ebony

BENJAMIN MOORE
Black

GLIDDEN
Exclamation Point

RALPH LAUREN
Nile

SHERWIN-WILLIAMS
Caviar

VALSPAR
Chimney Smoke

BEHR
Jet Black

BENJAMIN MOORE
Day's End

GLIDDEN
Monument

RALPH LAUREN
Orion Grey

BENJAMIN MOORE
Whale Gray

VALSPAR
Forest Shadow

BLACKS & GRAYS ....

BEHR
Market Tavern

BENJAMIN MOORE
Dior Gray

GLIDDEN
Olive Black

RALPH LAUREN
Seaweed

SHERWIN-WILLIAMS
Foggy Day

VALSPAR
Gray Frieze

SHERWIN-WILLIAMS
Thunderous

GLIDDEN
Tadpole

BEHR
Sled

BENJAMIN MOORE
Ebony King

GLIDDEN
Pebble Mosaic

RALPH LAUREN
Turret Stair

SHERWIN-WILLIAMS
Garden Gate

VALSPAR
Low River

BEHR
Stovepipe

VALSPAR
Silver Leaf

WHITES & OFF-WHITES..

BEHR
Arctic Ermine

BENJAMIN MOORE
Acadia White

GLIDDEN
Antique White

SHERWIN WILLIAMS
White Flour

RALPH LAUREN
Aloe Blossom

SHERWIN-WILLIAMS
Aria Ivory

VALSPAR
Antique White

BEHR
Bristol

BENJAMIN MOORE
Balboa Mist

GLIDDEN
Blessed Day

RALPH LAUREN
Beeswax

SHERWIN-WILLIAMS
Diamond

VALSPAR
Classic White

BEHR
Celestial Glow

BENJAMIN MOORE
Chantilly Lace

GLIDDEN
Blue Magic

WHITES & OFF-WHITES

RALPH LAUREN
Cameo

SHERWIN-WILLIAMS
Lilac Essence

VALSPAR
Constellation

BEHR
China Cup

BENJAMIN MOORE
Lily White

GLIDDEN
Crisp Linen

RALPH LAUREN
Cape Blanco

SHERWIN-WILLIAMS
Moderate White

VALSPAR
Dove White

BEHR
Coastal Fog

BENJAMIN MOORE
Ocean Air

GLIDDEN
Crystal

RALPH LAUREN
Deep Cream

SHERWIN-WILLIAMS
Off White

VALSPAR
Early Morn

BEHR
Cottonfield

BENJAMIN MOORE
Simply White

GLIDDEN
Everfrost

RALPH LAUREN
Design Studio White

SHERWIN-WILLIAMS
Pearly White

VALSPAR
March Breeze

BEHR
Cozy Cottage

BENJAMIN MOORE
Titanium

GLIDDEN
Gallery White

RALPH LAUREN
Gauze

SHERWIN-WILLIAMS
Twinkle

VALSPAR
Naivete

BEHR
Intimate White

BENJAMIN MOORE
White Dove

GLIDDEN
Vapor

RALPH LAUREN
Pocket Watch White

SHERWIN-WILLIAMS
Wedding White

resource guide

The following list of manufacturers and associations is meant to be a general guide to additional industry and product-related sources. It is not intended as a listing of products and manufacturers represented by the photographs in this book.

MANUFACTURERS & DISTRIBUTORS

UNITED STATES

Above View
414-744-7118
www.aboveview.com
Makes ornamental ceiling tiles.

Ace Hardware
866-290-5334
www.acehardware.com
A national chain of independently owned hardware stores.

Acme Sponge & Chamois Co., Inc.
800-937-3222
www.acmesponge.com
Distributes natural-sponge and chamois products worldwide.

Allerdice Building Supplies
518-584-5533
www.allerdice.com
Distributes paint and paint supplies.

Ampersand Art Supply
800-822-1939
www.ampersandart.com
Manufactures fine-art panels and related accessories.

Amtico
800-268-4260
www.amtico.com
Manufactures vinyl flooring.

Arts & Crafts by Rayson
800-526-1526
www.artsandcraftsbyrayson.com
Manufactures a variety of arts and crafts products.

Ballard Designs
800-536-7551
www.ballarddesigns.com
An online and catalog source for decorative accessories, including boxes and baskets.

Bassett Furniture
877-525-7070
www.bassettfurniture.com
Manufactures upholstered furniture and casegoods.

Behr
800-854-0133
www.behr.com
Manufactures paint, varnishes, and related products.

Benjamin Moore & Co.
800-344-0400
www.benjaminmoore.com
Manufactures paint, stains, and varnishes.

Bestt Liebco Corp.
800-547-0780
www.besttliebco.com
Manufactures painting tools, such as brushes and rollers.

Blue Mountain Wallcoverings, Inc.
866-563-9872
www.ihdg.com
Manufactures wallcoverings under the brand names Imperial, Sunworthy, Katzenbach & Warren, and Sanitas.

Brewster Wallcovering Co.
800-366-1700
www.brewsterwallcovering.com
Manufactures wallpaper, fabrics, and borders.

Calico Corners
800-213-6366
www.calicocorners.com
A national retailer specializing in fabric. In-store services include design consultation and custom window-treatment fabrication.

Canvas Concepts
800-869-7220
www.canvasconcepts.com
Manufactures pre-stretched colored canvases.

Central Fireplace
800-248-4681
www.centralfireplace.com
Manufactures freestanding and zero-clearance fireplaces.

Chroma
717-626-8866
www.chromaonline.com
Manufactures art supplies.

resource guide

Colker Co.
800-533-6561
www.colkercompany.com/decorative_arts.
html
Manufactures natural sea sponges and cloths.

Congoleum Corp.
609-584-3601
www.congoleum.com
Manufactures resilient, high-pressure plastic-laminate
flooring.

Corian, a division of DuPoint
800-906-7765
www.corian.com
Manufactures solid-surfacing material.

Couristan, Inc.
800-223-6186
www.couristan.com
Manufactures natural and synthetic carpets and rugs.

DaVinci Paint Co.
800-553-8755
www.davincipaints.com
Manufactures artist's paints, brushes, and knives.

Delta
800-423-4135
www.deltacrafts.com
Manufactures paint, stamps, and stencils.

Dick Blick
800-828-4548
www.dickblick.com
Sells acrylic, ceramic, fabric paints, universal tints, and art
supplies.

Dunn-Edwards
888-337-2468
www.dunnedwards.com
Manufactures paint and related products.

Dutch Boy
800-828-5669
www.dutchboy.com
Manufactures paint and related products.

Ethan Allen Furniture
888-324-3571
www.ethanallen.com
Manufactures and sells upholstered furniture and casegoods. Professional interior advice, including color consultation, is offered at Ethan Allan retail stores.

Fe Fi Faux
www.fefifaux.com
Manufactures trompe l'oeil wall murals and stencil designs.

Fine Paints of Europe
800-332-1556
www.finepaintsofeurope.com
Manufactures fine brushes, brushing putty, and alkyd paints.

Florida Tile
800-352-8453
www.floridatile.com
A distributor and manufacturer of ceramic wall and floor tile.

Formica Corporation
800-367-6422
www.formica.com
Manufactures plastic laminate, solid-surfacing material,
metal, and veneers.

Fuller O'Brien
www.fullerpaint.com
Manufactures primers, paints, and wood stains for interior
and exterior applications. The brand is specifically manufactured for and sold in the western United States.

Gautier
954-975-3303
www.gautierusa.com
Manufactures furniture.

Glidden
800-454-3336
www.glidden.com
Manufactures paint and related products.

Grumbacher
800-628-1910
www.grumbacherart.com
Manufactures conventional oil and water-soluble paints.

Houston Art, Inc.
800-898-7224
www.houstonart.com
Manufactures metallic powders, thinners, and other art supplies.

Hunter Douglas, Inc.
800-789-0331
www.hunterdouglas.com
Manufactures shades, blinds, and shutters. Its Web site directs you to designers, dealers, and installers.

Ikea
www.ikea.com
Manufactures furniture and home-organization accessories.

Jamestown Distributors
800-497-0010
www.jamestowndistributors.com
Distributes alkyd paints and other supplies.

Jerry's Artarama
800-827-8478
www.jerrysartarama.com
Distributes sponges, combs, graining tools, and specialty supplies.

Jian & Ling Bamboo
757-368-2060
www.jianlingbamboo.com
Manufactures vertical- and horizontal-cut bamboo flooring.

J.W. Etc.
361-887-6600
www.jwetc.com
Manufactures varnish, wood filler, and opaque primer.

Kemiko Concrete Products
903-587-3708
www.kemiko.com
Manufactures acid stains for concrete flooring and other concrete products. Creates decorative concrete floors.

Laticrete International, Inc.
800-243-4788
www.laticrete.com
Manufactures epoxy grout.

La-Z-Boy
www.la-z-boy.com
Manufactures furniture.

Lowe's
800-445-6937
www.lowes.com
A national home-improvement retailer.

Loew-Cornell. Inc.
866-227-9206
www.loew-cornell.com
Manufactures artist's brushes and accessories.

Magically Magnetic
724-352-3747
www.lyt.com
Manufactures magnetic paint.

Mannington
www.mannington.com
Manufactures wood and resilient-vinyl flooring.

Mark James Designs
www.markjamesdesign.com
Manufactures wall decals.

Masterchem Industries
866-744-6371
www.kilz.com
Manufactures primer.

Minwax
800-523-9299
www.minwax.com
Manufactures wood stains, fillers, and finishes.

My Perfect Color
www.myperfectcolor.com
A Web site that offers matches of over 100,000 colors across more than 100 paint brands.

Olde Century Colors
800-222-3092
www.oldecenturycolors.com
Manufactures paints and varnishes.

resource guide

Olympic Paints and Stains
800-441-9695
www.olympic.com
Manufactures paints and stains.

Palmer Paint Products
800-521-1383
www.palmerpaint.com
Manufactures paint products for general craft purposes.

Pearl Paint
800-451-7327
www.pearlpaint.com
Distributes a wide range of fine-art products, including paints and brushes.

Plaid Industries
800-842-4197
www.plaidonline.com
Manufactures craft-related products, including paints, stamps, and stencils.

PPG Pittsburgh Paints
800-441-9695
www.pittsburghpaints.com
Manufactures paints.

Pratt & Lambert
800-289-7728
www.prattandlambert.com
Manufactures paint, stains, and other related products.

Purdy Corp.
503-547-0780
www.purdycorp.com
Manufactures brushes.

Ralph Lauren Home
888-475-7674
www.ralphlaurenhome.com
Manufactures paint in addition to home furnishings.

Seabrook Wallcoverings, Inc.
800-238-9152
www.seabrookwallpaper.com
Manufactures borders and wallcoverings.

Sheffield Bronze Paint
216-481-8330
www.sheffieldbronze.com
Manufactures universal tints.

Sherwin-Williams
216-566-2284
www.sherwin-williams.com
Manufactures paints and finishes.

Solo Horton Brushes, Inc.
800-969-7656
www.solobrushes.com
Manufactures artist's and utility brushes.

Sonoma Cast Stone
888-807-4234
www.sonomastone.com
Designs and builds concrete sinks and countertops.

Springs Window Fashions
877-792-0002
www.springswindowfashions.com
Manufactures window treatments.

The Home Depot
800-553-3199
www.homedepot.com
A national home-improvement retailer.

3M
888-364-3577
www.3m.com
Manufactures sandpaper, adhesives, and other products.

T.J. Ronan Paint Corp.
800-247-6626
www.ronanpaints.com
Manufactures specialty paints.

True Value
www.truevalue.com
A national hardware retailer.

U.S. Art Quest
800-766-0728
www.usartquest.com
Manufactures art supplies, including paints and adhesives.

Valspar Corp.
800-845-9061
www.valspar.com
Manufactures paint, stains, and coatings.

Victoria Larsen
425-258-6812
www.victorialarsen.com
Manufactures stencils and stencil-making supplies.

West River Natural Paints
www.westriverpaints.com
Produces low-VOC, natural paint.

Wilsonart International
800-433-3222
www.wilsonart.com
Manufactures plastic laminate and solid-surfacing
material.

Winsor & Newton
800-445-4278
www.winsornewton.com
Manufactures artists' paints.

York Wallcoverings
717-846-4456
www.yorkwall.com
Manufactures borders and wallcoverings.

Zinsser Co, Inc.
732-469-8100
www.zinsser.com
Manufactures wallcovering-removal products, primers,
and sealants.

CANADA
General Paint
888-301-4454
www.generalpaint.com
Manufactures paint, architectural coatings, and wallpaper.

Nour Trading Co.
800-686-6687
www.nour.com
Manufactures professional painting tools.

Para Paints
800-461-7272
www.para.com
Manufactures paint, stains, and varnishes.

FAUX FINISHERS

Artistic Designs by Deidre
518-475-7973
www.adbydeidre.com
Fine artist and faux finisher.

Esmond Lyons
518-307-5929
elyons3@nycap.rr.com
Decorative and fine-art painter.

ASSOCIATIONS

UNITED STATES
American Society of Interior Designers (ASID)
202-546-3480
www.asid.org
An organization of professional interior designers.

The Color Association of the United States
212-947-7774
www.colorassociation.com
An organization that forecasts color trends.

INTERNATIONAL
**International Furnishings and Design Association
(IDFDA)**
610-535-6422
www.ifda.com
An alliance of professionals representing the industries that
constitute the universe of home furnishings and design.

Canadian Crafts Federation
905-891-5928
www.canadiancraftsfederation.ca
A national organization that represents Canadian
craft councils.

glossary

Accent color. Contrasting color used in small proportions to draw the eye and add interest.

Accent lighting. A type of directional lighting that highlights an area or object to emphasize that aspect of a room's character.

Accessible designs. Designs that accommodate persons with physical disabilities.

Adaptable designs. Designs that can be easily changed to accommodate a person with disabilities.

Acetate. The plastic-sheet material used for cutting stencils.

Acrylic. A water-based plastic polymer that acts as the binder in acrylic paints.

Acrylic varnish. A coating that contains the same medium used to make water-soluble paints and glazes.

Advancing colors. The warm colors. As with dark colors, they seem to advance toward you.

Alizarin crimson. One of the basic pigments, alizarin crimson is synthetically derived from coal tar and ranges from scarlet to maroon.

Alkyd paints. Paints with artificial resins (alkyds) forming their binder; often imprecisely called "oil-based" paints. Alkyds have replaced the linseed oil formerly used as a binder in oil-based paint.

Ambient lighting. General illumination that surrounds a room and is not directional.

Analogous colors. Two or more colors located next to one another on the color wheel.

Analogous Scheme. See *Harmonious color scheme.*

Antiquing. Any technique used to make a painted surface look old; usually refers to a thin glaze that is applied to a surface, allowing the undercoat to show through.

Art Deco. A decorative style that was based on geometric forms. It was popular during the 1920s and 1930s.

Art Nouveau. A late-nineteenth-century decorative style that was based on natural forms. It was the first style to reject historical references and create its own design vocabulary, which was ornamental and included stylized curved details.

Arts and Crafts. An architectural and decorative style that began in England during the late nineteenth century, where it was known as the Aesthetic Movement. Lead by William Morris, the movement rejected industrialization and encouraged fine craftsmanship and simplicity in design.

Artist's acrylics. Paints that contain pigments suspended in acrylic resin, similar to latex paint but of much higher quality.

Artist's brushes. Fine-tipped brushes for intricate work.

Artist's oils. The tube or oil-stick paint associated with fine-art paintings. They consist of pigments suspended in linseed oil.

Backlighting. Illumination coming from a source behind or at the side of an object.

Backsplash. The vertical part at the rear and sides of a countertop that protects the adjacent wall.

Base coat. The first coat of paint, which seals the surface.

Binder. A viscous, pliant material that holds pigments in suspension and makes them adhere to surfaces—the bulk of what makes up paint.

Blender brushes. Specialty brushes used to blend and soften all types of wet surfaces.

Box pleat. A double pleat, underneath which the edges fold toward each other.

Boxing. Pouring all paint of the same color and formula into one large container and then mixing it together to eliminate minor variations in color between cans.

Burled wood. Wood from a gnarled, knotty part of a tree, giving it a curved and irregular grain pattern.

Burnt sienna. One of the native colors, this is a deep, rich rust-red made from calcined raw sienna.

Burnt umber. One of the native colors, burnt umber is a dark reddish brown made from calcined raw umber.

Breccia marble. Marble that is composed of sharp fragments cemented together.

Built-in. Any element, such as a bookcase or cabinetry, that is built into a wall or an existing frame.

Cabriole. A double-curve or reverse S-shaped furniture leg that leads down to an elaborate foot (usually a ball-and-claw type).

Cadmium orange. One of the basic pigments, cadmium orange is made from cadmium sulfide and cadmium selenide.

Candlepower. The luminous intensity of a beam of light (total luminous flux) in a particular direction, measured in units called candelas.

Casegoods. A piece of furniture used for storage, including cabinets, dressers, and desks.

Casein paint. An old-fashioned paint made by mixing pigments with milk solids. Casein paint is seldom used except on furniture where a faded look is desired.

Chair rail. Trim running along a wall at chair height to prevent the moving of furniture from damaging the wall. Also known as a dado rail.

Cheesecloth. A loosely woven cotton gauze used to create many different textures in a finish, as well as to blend and smooth all paint techniques.

glossary

Cheesecloth distressing. The process of blending and softening paint strokes and colors by pouncing bunched-up cheesecloth over the wet surface.

China bristles. Another term for bristles made from boar hair.

Chroma. See *Intensity.*

Chrome green. A variety of green pigments made from chrome yellow and iron (Prussian) blue.

Chrome orange. One of the basic pigments, this orange-red pigment is made from lead chromate and lead oxides.

Chrome yellow. One of the basic pigments, this yellow pigment is made from lead chromate combined with lead sulfate.

Clear topcoat. A transparent finishing layer of protection applied on top of a painted finish.

Clearance. The amount of space between two fixtures, the centerlines of two fixtures, or a fixture and an obstacle, such as a wall.

Code. A locally or nationally enforced mandate regarding structural design, materials, plumbing, or electrical systems that state what you can or cannot do when you build or remodel.

Color scheme. A group of colors used together to create visual harmony in a space.

Color washing. Random layers of thin glaze that are blended to produce a faded, uneven look similar to that of whitewash or distemper.

Color wheel. A pie-shaped diagram showing the range and relationships of pigment. The three primary colors are equidistant, with secondary and tertiary colors placed between them.

Combing. Any paint technique that involves marking narrow lines of color on a surface. Also called "strié" or "dragging." Combing techniques that specifically intend to imitate natural wood grains are called "wood-graining" techniques.

Complementary colors. Colors located opposite one another on the color wheel.

Contemporary. Any modern design (after 1920) that does not contain traditional elements.

Contrast. The art of assembling colors with different values and intensities to create visual harmony in a color scheme.

Cool colors. The greens, blues, and violets.

Crackle glaze. Water-based glaze used under paint to create a peeling effect.

Cutters. Short, stiff-bristled brushes used to cut in lines, such as in corners and around trim.

Decoupage. French term for the technique of pasting and varnishing paper or fabric.

Deglossing. Roughing up a surface before painting so that it has "tooth," a texture that grabs paint.

Dimmer switch. A switch that can vary the intensity of the light source it controls.

Distemper. An old-fashioned type of interior paint made with pigments and a glue binder.

Distressing. Imitating wear and tear by rubbing down a surface.

Double-split complementaries. Colors on either side of two complementary colors on the color wheel.

Dragging. See *Combing.*

Dusting brushes. Soft, medium-length brushes used for combing, stippling, and softening textures.

Earth tones. The natural colors of earth; browns and beiges.

Eggshell. A thin, brittle semi-matte paint finish.

Enamel. Paint with finely ground pigments and a high binder content so that it dries to a hard gloss or semi-gloss finish.

Faux. French for "false"—used to describe any technique in which paint imitates another substance, such as wood or stone.

Faux finish. A decorative paint technique that imitates a pattern found in nature. An example would be a painted rendition of marble.

glossary

Federal. An architectural and decorative style popular in America during the early nineteenth century, featuring delicate ornamentation, often depicting swags and urns, and symmetrically arranged rooms.

Ferrule. The metal part of a paintbrush that attaches the bristles to the handle.

Fittings. The plumbing devices that bring water to the fixtures, such as faucets.

Flags. A word describing bristles with split ends, which help hold the paint.

Flogging brush. Wide, long-bristled brush used to texture surfaces by dragging or slapping wet paint or glaze. Also called a "dragger."

Fluorescent lighting. A glass tube coated on the interior with phosphor, a chemical compound that emits light when activated by ultraviolet energy. Air in the tube is replaced with a combination of argon gas and a small amount of mercury.

Focal point. The dominant element in a room or design, usually the first to catch your eye.

Foot-candle. A unit that is used to measure brightness. A foot-candle is equal to one lumen per square foot of lighted surface.

Framed cabinet. A cabinet with a full frame across the face of the cabinet box.

Frameless cabinet. A cabinet without a face frame. It may also be called a "European-style" cabinet.

Fresco. A picture created historically by painting onto wet plaster. Today the term is used to describe any picture painted onto a wall.

Frieze. Lateral band decorated differently from the rest of a room, usually high on a wall.

Full-spectrum light. Light that contains the full range of wavelengths that can be found in daylight, including invisible radiation (ultraviolet and infrared) at each end of the visible spectrum.

Georgian. An architectural and decorative style popular in America during the late eighteenth century, with rooms characterized by the use of paneling and other woodwork, and bold colors.

Gilding. Decorative technique giving a metallic appearance.

Glaze. A paint or colorant mixed with a transparent medium and diluted with a thinner compatible with the medium.

Gloss. A shiny finish that reflects the maximum amount of light.

Gothic Revival. An architectural and decorative style popular during the mid-nineteenth century. It romanticized the design vocabulary of the medieval period, using elements such as pointed arches and trefoils (three-leaf motifs).

Graining combs. Flexible steel or plastic combs that come in a variety of sizes and are used to striate and grain surfaces.

Greek Revival. An architectural and decorative style that drew inspiration from ancient Greek designs. It is characterized by the use of pediments and columns.

Grit paper. Another name for sandpaper—an abrasive paper used to smooth surfaces.

Harmonious color scheme. Also called "analogous," a combination focused on neighboring hues on the color wheel. The shared underlying color generally gives such schemes a coherent flow.

Harmonizing colors. Neighboring colors on the color wheel.

High-gloss finish. Paint with a shiny finish, usually oil-based.

Heart grain. Wood with a V-shaped grain pattern.

Hue. Synonym for color. Used most often to describe the color family to which a color belongs.

Incandescent lighting. A bulb (lamp) that converts electric power into light by passing electric current through a filament of tungsten wire.

Inlay. A decoration, usually consisting of stained wood, metal, ceramic or stone tile, or mother-of-pearl, that is set into the surface of an object in a pattern and finished flush.

Indirect lighting. A more subdued type of lighting that is not head-on, but rather reflected against another surface such as a ceiling.

Intensity. The brightness or dullness of a color. Also referred to as a color's purity or saturation.

Intermediate colors. Colors made by mixing equal amounts of one primary and one secondary color, such as red-orange and blue-green.

Japan colors. Concentrated oil-based colorants that are used for tinting alkyd paints and solvent-soluble glazes. Japan colors have an intense, flat color and will dry quickly.

Jasper. An opaque form of natural quartz that is usually yellow, brown, red, or green.

Lacquer. A protective clear finish, applied in several thin coats.

Lampblack. One of the native colors, lampblack is a deep black made from nearly pure carbon (containing some oil and tar impurities).

Latex paints. Paints that contain acrylic or vinyl resins or a combination of the two. High-quality latex paints contain 100-percent acrylic resin. Latex paints are water-soluble; that is, they can be thinned and cleaned up with water.

Leveling. The ability of a paint to smooth out after application so that it shows no brush or roller marks when it is dry.

Liming. Decorative technique of applying liming wax to create a soft, aged-looking finish.

Lining brushes. Thin, flexible, long-bristled brushes that are used for fine lining and detail work.

Linseed oil. An oil derived from flax seed that is used in oil-based paints and varnishes.

Lumen. The measurement of a source's light output—the quantity of visible light.

glossary

Matte finish. Also called "flat"—a dull, unshiny finish.

Mineral spirits. A petroleum distillate used as a solvent for alkyd-based paint.

Molding. An architectural band used to trim a line where materials join or create a linear decoration. It is typically made of wood, plaster, or a polymer.

Morocco leather. A soft and expensive leather made from the skin of goats tanned with sumac; by extension, a paint technique imitating it.

Mottler. A flat-ended brush used to make textures in glazed surfaces.

Mylar. A trademarked name for a strong but thin polyester film, often with a metallic pigmentation.

Nap. A soft or fuzzy surface on fabric such as a paint roller cover.

Native colors. The basic inorganic pigments that are derived from pigmented earth that has been colored by minerals and used to make the basic colors found in artist's oil paints. Those colors include: burnt sienna, burnt umber, lampblack, raw sienna, raw umber, and yellow ochre.

Negative technique. Any decorative painting technique that involves removing paint from a surface while it is still wet. See *Positive technique.*

Neoclassic. Any revival of the ancient styles of Greece and Rome, particularly during the late eighteenth and early nineteenth centuries.

Oil-based paint. A hard-wearing paint made from alkyd resin.

Oil varnish. See *Varnish.*

Overglaze. A thin glaze added as a final step to a finish. It can be the original glaze thinned somewhat or a new, thinner glaze in another color.

Overgrainers. Long, flat-bristled brushes used to apply paint detail, generally on dry, previously grained surfaces.

Palette. A set of colors in a scheme.

Palette knife. An artist's knife with a dull, flexible blade, used for mixing paints on a palette.

Panel. A flat, rectangular piece of material that forms part of a wall, door, or cabinet.

Parchment. An animal skin used for writing or paper made in imitation of it; by extension, the decorative finish that has a similar appearance.

Pastel. A color to which a lot of white has been added to make it pale in value.

Pattern matching. To align a repeating pattern when joining together two pieces of fabric or wallpaper.

Pediment. A triangular piece found over doors, windows, and occasionally mantles. It also refers to a low-pitched gable on the front of a building.

Peninsula. A countertop, with or without a base cabinet, that is connected at one end to a wall or another counter and extends outward, providing access on three sides.

Picture rail. Molding high on a wall from which frames can be hung.

Pigment. The substances that give paint color. Pigments are derived from natural or synthetic materials that have been ground into fine powders.

Polyurethane. A plastic resin, which makes a good topcoat for most types of paint except artist's oils. Thin it with mineral spirits or with water if water-based polyurethane.

Positive technique. Any painting technique that involves adding paint to a surface, which creates more depth. See *Negative technique.*

Primary colors. Red, yellow, and blue; the three colors in the visible spectrum that cannot be broken down into other colors. In various combinations and proportions, they make all other colors.

Primer. A coating that prepares surfaces for painting by making them more uniform in texture and giving them tooth.

Quaternary colors. Colors made by mixing two tertiary colors.

Ragging off. The technique in which paint is pulled from a surface using a bunched-up cloth. Sometimes called "cheeseclothing."

Ragging on. The technique in which paint is applied to a surface using a bunched-up cloth.

Rag-rolling off. A technique in which paint or glaze is removed from a surface using a rolled-up piece of cloth that is lifted off in a rhythmic pattern.

Raw sienna. One of the native colors, raw sienna is an earthy yellow-brown made from clay containing iron and aluminum oxides, which is found in the area of Tuscany around Siena.

Raw umber. One of the native colors, raw umber is a cool brown made from a clay containing iron oxides and manganese dioxide, originally from the Italian region of Umbria.

Receding colors. The cool colors. They make surfaces seem farther from the eye.

Red ochre. A basic pigment, it is red tinged slightly with violet, made from clay containing iron oxide.

Refined white beeswax. Derived from natural beeswax, this product produces an elegant, lustrous finish that doesn't yellow.

Registration marks. Small holes cut into a stencil with more than one layer, which allow you to match up the different layers.

glossary

Resin. A category of solid or semi-solid, viscous substances, both natural (rosin, amber, copal) and synthetic (polyvinyl, polystyrene).

Round fitches. Round brushes with firm but flexible bristles. They are used for spattering, stippling, and stenciling.

Rust inhibitors. Chemicals added to special paints intended for metal surfaces that may corrode.

Satin finish. Paint finish that is mildly shiny with little glare. Also known as "semigloss."

Sealer. A product (for example, shellac) that seals porous surfaces by forming a durable, nonabsorbent barrier that prevents them from sucking up paint.

Sea sponge. The fibrous connective structure of a sea creature used to apply and remove paint. Not to be confused with the cellulose variety.

Secondary colors. Orange, green, and violet; the colors made by mixing equal amounts of two primary colors.

Semigloss. A slightly lustrous finish that reflects light and has an appearance somewhere between gloss and eggshell.

Shade. A color to which black has been added to make it darker.

Sheen. The quality of paint that reflects light.

Shellac. The secretion of a Southeast Asian insect dissolved in alcohol, which is used as a sealer. It comes in three colors: clear (sometimes labeled "white"); white-pigmented (also referred to as "opaque" and "chalked white"), and "orange" or "blond."

Snap time. The point at which a paint or glaze has begun to dull down and become tacky. After snap time, a paint cannot be worked without causing damage to the finish.

Solvent. A liquid capable of dissolving another substance (such as mineral spirits for alkyd paint and water for latex paint).

Spalter. A type of natural-bristle brush used for smoothing on alkyd paints.

Spattering. The technique of applying random dots of paint over a surface by striking a saturated brush or rubbing paint through a screen.

Split complementary. A color paired with the colors on either side of its complementary color on the color wheel.

Sponging. A paint technique that uses a natural sea sponge to apply or remove paint.

Staining. The technique of using oil- or water-based paints to add transparent color to wooden surfaces.

Stencil. A cut-out pattern. Complex stencils will have several overlapping patterns, and different colors are applied in layers after the previous coat dries.

Stippling. A paint technique that involves pouncing a special brush straight up and down over a surface, creating myriad tiny dots that blend together when viewed from a distance. Similar to the fine-art technique known as "pointillism."

Stippling brush. A blocky, stiff-bristled china brush used to stipple wet paints, glazes, and top coats.

Strié. See *Combing*.

Task lighting. Directional lighting that concentrates in specific areas for tasks, such as preparing food, applying makeup, reading, or doing crafts.

Tempera paint. A mixture of pigments and a water-soluble glutinous emulsion binder, often made from an oil extracted from egg yolks.

Terebene dryer. A substance (prepared from oil of turpentine) that can be added to alkyd-based paints (most often house paints) to speed drying.

Tertiary colors. Colors made by combining equal amounts of two secondary colors.

Texturing compounds. Substances that go into paints where a rough, grained, or dimensional quality is desired.

Thinner. A liquid that is mixed with paint to make it less thick, such as turpentine or white mineral spirits for alkyd-based paints and water for latex-based paints.

Tint. A color to which white has been added to make it lighter in value.

Titanium white. The most common white pigment, titanium white is a brilliant white that is synthetically derived from the metal titanium.

Tonal value. The lightness or darkness of a color.

Tone. A color to which gray has been added to change its value.

Tooth. The coarse quality of a surface (or a coating on a surface) that improves the performance, appearance, and longevity of paint.

Triad. Any three colors located equidistant from one another on the color wheel.

Track lighting. Lighting that utilizes a fixed band that supplies a current to movable light fixtures.

Trompe l'oeil. French for "fool the eye"—used to describe a painted surface that convincingly mimics reality.

Tufting. The fabric of an upholstered piece or a mattress that is drawn tightly to secure the padding, creating regularly spaced indentations.

Turpentine. A solvent made from distillate of pine resins, used as a thinner and cleaner for alkyd-based paints.

Ultramarine blue. One of the native colors, ultramarine blue is an intense blue originally made from crushed lapis lazuli, but now formulated from man-made pigments.

Undercoat. Protective layer of paint between primer and top coat.

Universal tints. Pigments that are combined with ethylene glycol and a small amount of water. They are usable in both water- and alkyd-based paints and glaze mediums.

Value. The lightness (tint or pastel) and darkness (shade) of a color.

Value scale. A graphic tool used to show the range of values between pure white and true black.

Varnish. The traditional top coat used in decorative painting, consisting of an oil-based paint with a solvent and an oxidizing or evaporating binder, which leaves behind a thin, hard film.

Vehicle. See *Binder.*

Vermillion red. One of the basic pigments, vermilion red is a brilliant pure red made from mercuric sulphide.

Visible spectrum. The bands of hues created when sunlight passes through a prism.

Warm colors. Generally, the reds, oranges, and yellows; often including the browns.

Wash. A thinned-out latex or acrylic paint.

Water-based polyurethane. A sealer made from polyurethane resins that is water soluble.

Wavelength. The means of measuring the electromagnetic spectrum; the portion of this spectrum that is visible as light has waves that measure between 4,000 and 7,000 angstroms, with red having the longest waves and violet the shortest.

Wet edge. A margin of wet paint or glaze. Leaving a wet edge creates a seamless blend between sections.

Wood graining. A painting technique that seeks to resemble wood by imitating the lines or growth rings found in cut lumber.

Wood stain. A translucent combination of solvent (either water- or alkyd-based) and pigment, usually in colors imitating natural wood, which allow some of the wood's natural color and its grain to be visible.

Yellow ochre. One of the native colors, yellow ochre is a mustard-yellow made from clay containing iron oxide.

Zinc white. A common white pigment, it is brilliant and derived from the metal zinc.

index

index

designer & photo credits

All photography by Mark Samu.

page 1: design: Pascucci Deslisle Design **page 2:** design: Esmond Lyons **page 6:** design: Mercedes Courland Design **pages 8–9:** design: Maria Billis Designs **page 10:** design: Lucianna Samu Design **page 11:** design: Pascucci Deslisle Design **pages 12–13:** design: Lucianna Samu Design **page 14:** design: Robert Storm AIA **page 15:** design: Lucianna Samu Design **page 16:** *top* design: Lucianna Samu Design; *bottom* design: Steven Goldgram Design **page 17:** design: Marlaina Teich Designs **page 18:** design: Lynn Gerhard Design **page 19:** design: Ann Stillman O'Leary, Evergreen House Interiors **page 21:** design: Robert Storm AIA **page 22:** design: Lucianna Samu Design **page 23:** *top* design: Noli Design; *bottom* design: Robert Storm AIA **pages 24–25:** design: Kate Singer Home **page 26:** design: Noli Design **page 27:** *left* design: EC Designs; *right* design: Marlaina Teich Designs **page 28:** design: Robert Storm AIA **page 29:** *top left* design: Lynn Gerhard Design; *right* design: Pascucci Deslisle Design **pages 30–31:** design: Kate Singer Home **pages 32–33:** design: Carpen House **pages 34–35:** design: Beach Glass Interior Design **page 36:** *top left* design: EKB Interiors; *bottom left* design: Lucianna Samu Design **page 37:** *top left* design: EKB Interiors; *top right* design: Lucianna Samu Design; *bottom right* design: Esmond Lyons; *bottom left* design: Donald Billinkoff AIA **pages 38–39:** design: EKB Interiors **pages 42–43:** design: EKB Interiors **pages 44–47:** design: Lucianna Samu Design **pages 50–51:** design: Donald Billinkoff AIA **pages 52–53:** *left & center* design: Esmond Lyons; *right* design: Lucianna Samu Design **page 55:** *bottom* design: EKB Interiors **pages 56–57:** design: EKB Interiors **page 58:** *top right* design: Maria Billis Designs **page 59:** *top left* design: Lucianna Samu Design; *top right* design/architect: Doug Moyer AIA; *bottom right* design: Charles Reilly Design; *bottom left* design: Noli Design **pages 62–63:** design: Maria Billis Designs **pages 64–65:** design: Lucianna Samu Design **page 66:** design/architect: Doug Moyer AIA **pages 72–73:** design: Esmond Lyons **page 75:** design: Noli Design **pages 76–77:** design: Charles Reilly Design **pages 78–79:** design: Keith Baltimore Design **page 80:** *top right* design: EKB Interiors; *bottom right* design: Lucianna Samu Design; *bottom left* design: Kate Singer Home **page 81:** *top left* design: Keith Baltimore Design; *top right* design: Schuyler Pond; *bottom right* design: Lee Najman Design; *bottom center & left* design: Robert Storm AIA **pages 84–85:** design: EKB Interiors **pages 86–87:** design: Keith Baltimore Design **page 88:** design: Schuyler Pond **page 89:** *top* design: Benvenuti & Stein **pages 90–91:** *left* design: Kate Singer Home; *right* design: EKB Interiors **pages 92–93:** design: Lucianna Samu Design **pages 94–97:** design: Robert Storm AIA **page 98:** design: Lee Najman Design **pages 100–101:** design: Robert Storm AIA **page 102:** design: Peter Cook AIA **page 103:** design: Robert Storm AIA **page 104:** design: Brian Shore AIA **page 105:** design: Robert Storm AIA **page 106:** design: Steven Goldgram Design **page 107:** design: Beverly Balk Design **page 108:** design: Artistic Designs by Deidre **page 109:** design: Brian Shore AIA **page 110:** *top right* design: Peter Cook AIA; *bottom right* design: EJR AIA **page 111:** *left* design: Robert Storm AIA; *top right* design/builder: Durst Construction; *bottom right* design: Donald Billinkoff AIA **pages 114–115:** design: Peter Cook AIA **pages 116–117:** *left* design: Maria Billis Designs; *center & right* design: EJR AIA **pages 118–119:** design: Robert Storm AIA **pages 120–121:** design/builder: Durst Construction **pages 122–123:** design: Donald Billinkoff AIA **pages 124–125:** design: Keith Baltimore Design **page 126:** *top left* design: Keith Baltimore Design; *top right* design: Maria Billis Designs; *bottom left* design: Pascucci Deslisle Design **page 127:** *top left* design: Pascucci Deslisle Design; *top right* design: Lucianna Samu Design; *bottom* design: Charles Reilly Design **pages 128–129:** design: Keith Baltimore Design **pages 130–131:** design: Maria Billis Designs **pages 132–133:** design: Pascucci Deslisle Design **pages 134–135:** design: Lucianna Samu Design **pages 136–137:** design: Pascucci Deslisle Design **pages 140–143:** design: Charles Reilly Design **pages 144–145:** design: Pascucci Deslisle Design **page 146:** *left* design: EKB Interiors; *top right* design: Esmond Lyons; *bottom right* design: Kate Singer Home **page 147:** *top left* design/builder: Bonacio Construction; *right* design: Pascucci Deslisle Design; *bottom left* design: Beach Glass Interior Design **pages 148–149:** design: EKB Interiors **pages 150–151:** design: Esmond Lyons **pages 152–153:** design: Kate Singer Home **page 154:** design: Bonacio Construction **page 155:** design: EKB Interiors **page 156:** design: Beach Glass Designs **page 157:** *top* design: Pascucci Deslisle Design; *bottom* design: Donald Billinkoff AIA **pages 158–159:** design: Pascucci Deslisle Design **page 189:** design: Beach Glass Designs **page 195:** design: Capital Construction **page 196:** design: Bonacio Construction **page 199:** design: Ann Stillman O'Leary, Evergreen House Interiors **page 200:** design: Kathryn Jessica Interiors

Have a home decorating or improvement project?
Look for these and other fine **Creative Homeowner**
books wherever books are sold

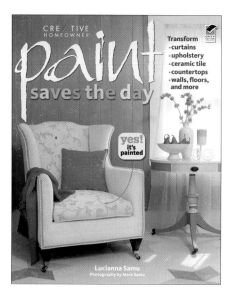

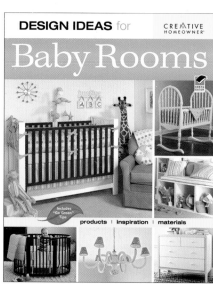

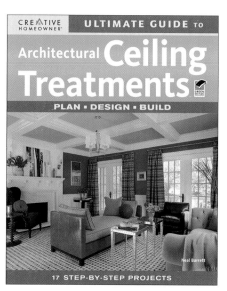

Paint Saves the Day
Over 275 color photos. 208 pp.;
8½" x 10⅞"
$19.95 (US) $23.95 (CAN)
BOOK #: CH279575

Design Ideas for Baby Rooms
350 color photos. 208 pp.;
8½" x 10⅞"
$19.95 (US) $23.95 (CAN)
BOOK #: CH279294

**Ultimate Guide to Architectural
Ceiling Treatments**
Over 530 color photos and illos. 192 pp.;
8½" x 10⅞"
$19.95 (US) $21.95 (CAN)
BOOK #: CH279286

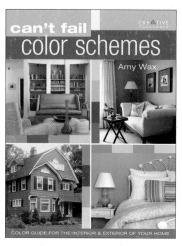

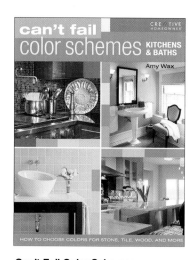

Can't Fail Color Schemes
300 color photos. 304 pp.;
7" x 9¼"
$19.95 (US) $24.95 (CAN)
BOOK #: CH279659

**Can't Fail Color Schemes—
Kitchens and Baths**
300 color photos. 304 pp.;
7" x 9¼"
$19.95 (US) $21.95 (CAN)
BOOK #: CH279648

Decorating to Go
200 color photos. 176 pp.;
6¼" x 9¼"
$12.95 (US) $15.95 (CAN)
BOOK #: CH279582

For more information and to order direct, go to www.creativehomeowner.com